Teaching
the Mildly
Handicapped
in the
Regular Classroom

Second Edition

Teaching the Mildly Handicapped in the Regular Classroom

Second Edition

James Q. Affleck
University of Washington

Sheila Lowenbraun
University of Washington

Anita Archer
University of Oregon

Charles E. Merrill Publishing Company
A Bell & Howell Company
Columbus   Toronto   London   Sydney

Published by Charles E. Merrill Publishing Company
A Bell & Howell Company
Columbus, Ohio 43216

This book was set in Times Roman.
Production Editor: Lucinda A. Peck.
Cover Design Coordination: Will Chenoweth.

Library of Congress Catalog Card Number: 79-91089

International Standard Book Number: 0-675-08132-7

Printed in the United States of America

1 2 3 4 5 6 7 8 9 10—85 84 83 82 81 80

Contents

Preface

In 1976 we used the term "mainstreaming" to describe the integration of mildly handicapped children into regular education programs. Although at that time there were court precedents for such action, and hints of trends toward increasing funds for these programs, mainstreaming remained optional and had no supporting empirical evidence of its educational efficacy.

Four years later, we still have no definitive research supportive of the efficacy of integrating handicapped students into regular classrooms. Nevertheless, since P.L. 94–142 has mandated this process, the lack of empirical support is a moot issue. This legal mandate has eclipsed the concept of "mainstreaming" with the more comprehensive "least restrictive environment idea." School districts no longer have sole authority to place handicapped students, but rather must involve parents and, if possible, the handicapped student himself as part of the Individualized Education Program (IEP).

Due to these sweeping changes in legislation regarding the education of handicapped children, we have revised TEACHING MILDLY HANDICAPPED CHILDREN IN REGULAR CLASSES. We have, however, tried to retain the *practical* emphasis of the book to assist elementary teachers with successfully integrating mildly handicapped students into their classes.

You will notice that we have substantially added materials to the second edition. We have doubled the coverage of assessment and task analysis since planning for teaching mildly handicapped children is of such critical concern to elementary teachers.

We have also included a new chapter on behavior management (Chapter 4) that occurs before the chapters concerning "what to teach." To make this chapter as useful to you as possible, we solicited the comments of elementary teachers and tried to address each one of their problems in managing handicapped children in their classrooms. You will note that the academic skills chapters have been substantially expanded to analyze carefully the steps of the instructional sequences.

Wherever possible we have updated our discussions to reflect the most recent legislation concerning the education of handicapped children. We doubt that further developments will modify these requirements from state to state, but the spirit of "mainstreaming" shall probably remain with us for some time to come. It is our modest hope that our book can make some positive impact on the better education of mildly handicapped children in regular classes.

As with all works, ours has been enhanced by the comments of professional reviewers. We give our thanks to Richard Cortright, National Education Association, Judith Grosenick, University of Missouri at St. Louis, and Judy Olson, University of Central Florida for their constructive reviews. Their contributions show on these pages.

J.A.

S.L.

A.A.

1

The Exceptional Child and Special Education

All human beings are unique. They differ from each other genetically, psychologically, physically, sociologically, and intellectually. Even identical twins with the same genetic characteristics, by virtue of being exposed to different experiences, develop characteristics unique to themselves. However, in spite of this uniqueness, most people still blend into the majority of the population. They are not outstandingly different, but rather contain their uniqueness within "normal" limits. Some parameters of human difference are easily quantifiable. We may measure such physical factors as weight, height, manual dexterity, strength, visual acuity, and hearing threshold, and then compare them with norms appropriate to the individual's age and sex. From these measures a quantitative picture of one individual's deviation from the average, or norm, is obtained. Such factors as intelligence, adaptive behavior, social adjustment, aggressiveness, and facility of speech and language are much harder to quantify in a meaningful way.

THE LABELING OF EXCEPTIONAL CHILDREN

A fine line somewhat arbitrarily placed on the continuum of human differences divides those significantly different "exceptional" individuals from their peers whose uniqueness falls within normal limits. Children of school age are particularly likely to be labeled as exceptional by one or more institutions of society through the process of education. Public Law 94-142 defines handicapped children as those who have been evaluated as being "mentally retarded, hard of hearing, deaf, speech impaired, visually handicapped, seriously emotionally disturbed, orthopedically

James Q. Affleck and Sheila Lowenbraun

impaired, other health impaired, deaf-blind, multihandicapped, or as having specific learning disabilities. . . '' and requiring special services (*Federal Register*, August 23, 1977, p. 42478). Traditionally, children who deviate below the normal mental range of the population on the basis of standardized intelligence test results have been labeled mentally retarded or mentally deficient. Children who deviate from the norm in physical characteristics include those who have specific neurological dysfunctions, are hard of hearing or deaf, are visually handicapped, deaf-blind, speech impaired, orthopedically impaired, or other health impaired. Children who deviate from the norm in social and emotional adjustment are often labeled emotionally disturbed or behaviorally disordered, while those who deviate only in learning performance are labeled learning disabled or another similar term.

How Labeling Should Affect Education

Labeling a child as exceptional is neither inherently good nor inherently evil. In the past, labeling has had a positive impact resulting in increased funds earmarked for remedial and special education. However, labeling has also been a means of excluding exceptional children from the mainstream of education and, in the case of more severely handicapped children, preventing them from receiving any educational services at all. The basis for providing special, more extensive, and more expensive educational services to exceptional children is the philosophical premise that each child has the right to receive help in developing to the limits of his capacity, including children who will never be self-sufficient. Those children who will probably require full-time custodial care for the rest of their lives must be provided educational services at their level of functioning, and children whose prognosis is death before reaching adulthood should have an education geared to their mental and physical capacities. The more extensive the disability or the more severe the educational handicap, the more extensive (and possibly expensive) the services should be.

A Bridge Between the Disability and the Norm

Most of the disabilities dealt with in special education are overt conditions that indicate a significant quantitative or qualitative deviation from the norm and are, with some exceptions, not "curable." Neither medicine nor psychology can modify the chromosomal abnormality of a Down's syndrome child, repair the hair cells in the cochlea of a sensori-neural hearing-impaired child, or change the brain of a child with cerebral palsy.

Lowenbraun and Affleck (1978) note that *disability* is an apparent physical or behavioral deviation from normal. It is, at least theoretically, observable and measurable. One can, for example, measure the degree of hearing loss through standard audiometric tests; the degree of visual impairment through optometric examinations; and the degree of mental retardation through standardized intelligence tests and adaptive behavior scales. Somewhat less clearly, it is possible to measure the degree and type of emotional disturbance, using either projective techniques or behavioral objectives. The categories of disabling conditions are roughly described in the federal or various state lists of eligibility characteristics for children in special education.

A *handicap* is not as easy to quantify since it results from the interaction of a disability or overt difference from the norm with society's expectations for adaptive behaviors in such areas as communication, locomotion, socialization, occupation, and self-direction *(Vineland Social Maturity Scale,* Doll, 1965). Society unconsciously and collectively places value on certain behaviors and degrades others. These values, which are culturally determined, are generally not articulated except when they are violated.

For example, society values the ability to speak articulately and clearly in the prevalent dialect (e.g., standard English). However, some accents are culturally determined to be acceptable and some are deemed unacceptable. A British accent is usually considered "high class;" a French accent is considered variously to be "cosmopolitan," "cute," or "sexy." However, a Mexican-American accent or a southern black dialect is usually considered "low class" or "uncultured." Thus, some people have spent much time and effort, largely unsuccessfully, trying to have black English taught in schools, and to convince people of the respectability of the black dialect.

Another value of society, also unarticulated unless violated, is the ability to dress appropriately in accordance with expectations for age, sex, and social situation. Others include the ability to display the proper emotions at the proper time, the ability to deal appropriately with bodily functions (e.g., to be toilet trained, not to masturbate in public, not to drool), and the ability to do adequate or above-average work in school or vocational situations.

Handicapped children differ from racial, religious, or cultural minorities in two important ways. First, handicapped children are usually not born into handicapped families. With certain exceptions, such as genetic deafness and perhaps "cultural–familial" retardation, handicapped children are born to parents who are normal and who did not anticipate having a deviant child. Thus, the children must bear the stigma of being handicapped within their families as well as within society. Second, handicapped children are by reason of their disability truly handicapped. While they can be taught to circumvent their disabilities to some extent or to use prosthetic aids to learning, they cannot be totally "unhandicapped" merely by placement in proximity to normal peers. In fact, except for those with short-term problems, it is unlikely that any educational technique will totally "cure" the disability and thus remove the handicaps associated with it (Lowenbraun & Affleck, 1978).

MEETING THE NEEDS OF CHILDREN

Handicaps can at times be lessened by prosthetic devices such as wheelchairs, corrective lenses, and hearing aids, or paramedical services such as physical and occupational therapy. One of the most important ways of lessening most handicaps is through appropriate educational techniques.

As has been stated, special education is not limited to a specific physical facility or "special class," but may occur in any environment including the regular classroom. Its primary characteristics in any situation should be that the education is tailored to the needs and abilities of the individual child. Both regular and special educators should strive to provide all exceptional children with as many skills as they are able to acquire which will lead them toward successful social and vocational integration into the mainstream of society. The sequence for providing such an individualized program includes the following components:

1. Prior to placement and periodically thereafter, a precise, educationally relevant diagnosis should be made which pinpoints the child's levels of achievement, any problems in helping the child learn, and the most appropriate educational goals, methods, and materials for ensuring success.

2. On the basis of this diagnosis, an individually prescribed instructional program is cooperatively formulated by the school, the parents or guardian, and, if appropriate, the child.

3. Throughout the program, the teacher precisely monitors the success or failure of the educational strategies used by collecting and analyzing data on the child's performance.

Special education adapts itself to the needs of individual children in three ways: by modifying educational goals, modifying educational methods and materials, and modifying the physical environment of education. We will examine briefly each of these modification processes.

Modifying the Goals of Education

The goals of regular education are the facilitation of economic, vocational, and social independence; active participation as a citizen in the affairs of the community, state and nation; and educational competence. A new emphasis in regular education is the development of "basic skills" necessary for coping with society's demands. For some exceptional children, these goals are inappropriate or impractical. As an example, for exceptional students who deviate greatly from the norm, educational goals might be the ability to:

wash and dress themselves appropriately
react appropriately to warning signs
use a toilet independently

In state and federal laws mandating an appropriate education for all handicapped children, a major requirement is the cooperative development of long-term educational goals by the school, the child's parents and, if appropriate, the child. These goals, which are individually determined, will reflect the best possible compromise between the goals of regular education and the child's unique pattern of strengths and handicaps. The goals will be modified throughout the child's educational program according to his/her performance in the school and community.

Modifying Educational Methods and Materials

Some exceptional children can learn approximately the same things as normal children of similar ability but must use different materials, devices, or sensory modalities to circumvent their handicaps. Blind children, for example, use such aids as raised maps and charts, Braille books, Braille typewriters, tactile arithmetic materials, and talking books to alleviate their communication handicap and enable them to progress more normally through school.

Hearing-impaired children may need special communication aids such as hearing aids and auditory training units to function optimally in a classroom. More severely hearing-impaired children may function best when given instruction in manual communication through fingerspelling and sign language. For some children, an interpreter who translates class activities to sign language for the child and translates the child's communication into oral language for the teacher and peers makes it possible for most of their education to be provided in the regular classroom, with supplementary instruction in speech and language.

Physically handicapped children may need special adaptive devices for mobility, such as braces, crutches, and electric wheelchairs, and for communication, such as specially adapted typewriters or communication boards, where responses can be indicated by nodding or pointing.

It is for these types of children that integration holds exceptional promise. Sometimes very small modifications—re–designing a bathroom door, providing an interpreter, or acquiring an electric wheelchair—are the main physical adaptations necessary to permit a child to be educated with his normal peers. Along with these physical adaptations, attitude adjustments must also develop to permit psychological as well as physical integration to occur.

Modifying the Physical Environment of Education

Sometimes the educational site itself must be modified to provide optimal services to exceptional children. Some children need educational services while they are in hospitals. Others need to be educated where occupational and physical therapy are available. Still others may be in residential care centers because of severe mental, physical, or emotional problems.

When exceptional children are educated at a facility that is not in or near the facility where normal children are being taught, the exceptional child may be further alienated from the very community he or she is being prepared to reenter. Let us examine the types of physical settings where exceptional children are being served, moving from the most segregated to the least segregated. The goal for each child should be service in the most normal environment possible.

Residential Facilities

Homebound instruction

Perhaps the most segregated form of educational service that has ever been offered to exceptional children is homebound instruction. Here a child is educated, usually on a part-time basis, by a teacher who comes to the home. This method is usually employed with chronically ill children, or those who are undergoing an extended convalescence. Conference telephones and other new media equipment designed to lessen the isolation of homebound instruction now enable homebound students to take part in class discussions taking place in a normal school. In some school districts, however, homebound instruction has also been used with severely emotionally disturbed children, cerebral palsied children, and the mentally retarded. Here, the motivation was often one of school district expedience; the district did not then have to provide transportation or physical facilities for the deviant child.

Institutions

Institutions for mentally retarded, emotionally disturbed, or socially maladjusted children usually have as primary goals: (1) the protection of the child from society,

(2) the protection of society from the child, and, in some cases, (3) the provision of custodial care. As an adjunct to these functions, some education may be provided, usually in a completely segregated facility. In the past, and in some institutions for the retarded today, the long-term (unstated) goal of institutional education was the production of a reasonably self-sufficient institutional resident, who might then work in the institution to help with the lower functioning residents and perform menial services on the institution grounds. More progressive institutions, such as the Rainier State School at Buckley, Washington, are now providing programmed re-entry into the community as part of their education.

Boarding schools

The incidence of hearing problems (deaf: 0.075%; hard-of-hearing: 0.5%) and blindness (0.1%) in the school-age population is much lower than for other types of exceptionality such as mental retardation (2.3%) and behavioral disability (2.0%) (Hallahan & Kauffman, 1978). Due to these low-incidence figures, the relatively easy identification of the problems of the deaf and blind, and the success of educating children with these handicaps, a network of publicly supported boarding schools for the deaf and blind sprang up very early in the history of the United States. Unlike institutions for the retarded, these schools had a primary educational purpose: that, after graduation, the students would enter the world of work and function independently in society.

At these facilities, which still exist in most states, students live at school, going home on weekends if they live close enough, or sometimes only for long vacations and during the summer months. There is usually little interaction between students at the school and the residents of the community. The school provides all needs, including religious instruction, recreation, and medical and dental service for children who do not go home regularly.

For children with low-incidence handicaps, the boarding school offers inter-action with other handicapped individuals, a complete array of diagnostic services, and a complete and sustained educational and vocational program geared to their exceptionality. In exchange for these benefits, the students are required to give up any potential interaction with normal peers, normal living with parents and family, and familiarity with their home community and the services it provides. It is questionable today whether the boarding school meets the letter or the spirit of federal legislation unless it provides systematic opportunity for interaction with normal peers.

Day Facilities

Special schools

In larger cities and suburban areas, enough handicapped children of certain categories exist to warrant the construction of special physical facilities for a given type of exceptional child or for several categories of handicapped children with common needs. Advantages of this type of setting are the same as those of boarding schools, with the added advantage of not isolating children from their parents, families, or community for long periods of time. Educationally, however, these children are still totally outside the mainstream and have no opportunity for interaction with normal peers. Additionally, they must often spend long periods each day being transported to and from school.

Special day classes

Special day classes for exceptional children are located on the campus of a school for nonhandicapped children. This administrative arrangement permits social inter-action by handicapped children with their normal peers in the lunchroom and on the playground, and allows participation in nonacademic classes and activities. All academic education, however, still takes place in isolation from the mainstream of public education.

Resource rooms

Resource rooms have recently come into use with mildly and moderately handi-capped children. Pupils are assigned to regular classrooms, and spend the majority of each day in these classes. For some academic work, however, they go to a re-source room where a special educator helps them with their specific areas of academic weakness. Emotionally disturbed children may also use this classroom as a place to go when their behavior in their regular classroom becomes unacceptable. Because the regular classroom teacher maintains overall responsibility for the ex-ceptional child's education, the child is considered to be integrated into the main-stream of education.

Itinerant teachers

In some cases, children need special service for only a small portion of the school day, or for a few days each week. To correct a minor articulation problem, for example, a speech therapist may be needed for only an hour or so per week. Such specialists are called itinerant teachers, since they often work in more than one school. Itinerant teachers often provide special auditory training, lipreading, and speech lessons to mildly hearing-impaired children; Braille lessons and mobility training to visually impaired children; and speech therapy to language-disordered children. Such specialists may also serve as consultants to the regular classroom teacher, and may be able to provide special materials and prosthetic aids for use during regular class instruction.

THE "LABELED" CHILD IN THE REGULAR CLASS

In the past decade there has been an increasing national movement toward "mainstreaming" mildly handicapped children. The common concept underlying these efforts is that mildly handicapped people must eventually find their places in adult society and that segregation in special classes has not accelerated their academic and social development to the level previously expected (Dunn, 1968). Though there is no empirical support for concluding that integration is superior to special class placement, the mainstreaming of handicapped children is being carried out rapidly and regular elementary and intermediate teachers are likely now to find handicapped children in their classrooms with increasing frequency.

Assistance to the Teacher

As mainstreaming of mildly handicapped students becomes more widely practiced, regular elementary and intermediate teachers will be expected to educate children with mild mental retardation, learning disabilities, and emotional disturbance as well as some with physical handicaps. In some cases, children already in the regular classroom may appear to the teacher to have these handicaps. However, the "labeled" child will have been clinically assessed and certified to be sufficiently handicapped to be eligible for special education services. Labeling a child as educable mentally retarded, learning disabled, or emotionally disturbed (or equivalent terms used in other states, for example in California, educationally handicapped) is a legal step necessary for gaining sufficient funds to provide additional special services for the child. Regular educators have a right to expect additional assistance if such handicapped children are placed in their classes. This assistance will usually take the form of specified help from special education resource personnel based in the regular elementary or intermediate school. Affleck, Lehning, and Brow (1973, p. 448) have provided the following sample job description of a primary level resource teacher.

The teacher will:

1. Assume total responsibility for individual diagnosis, program planning, and evaluation for all special education students placed in grades 1 through 3.
2. Assume primary responsibility for processing all referrals from teachers of grades 1 through 3, including meeting with the team leader regarding final action to be taken on each referral.
3. Team teach a minimum of two classes from grades 1 through 3 with the regular classroom teacher, sharing planning and materials preparation responsibilities.
4. Complete all required student reports for students from grades 1 through 3 to whom direct services are provided.
5. Prepare, present, and file staffing material for all special education students in grades 1 through 3.
6. Report to the parents of each special education student in grades 1 through 3 a minimum of four times during the school year, two reports to be via joint conferences with the regular classroom teacher.
7. Report to the parents of resource students when programs with each student are initiated and terminated, as well as during regular report periods while service is being given.

Affleck et al. (1973, p. 448) also provided a sample daily schedule that illustrates the type of service provided to the regular classroom teacher.

8:00-8:30	Team meetings/student staffings in resource center
8:30-8:45	Preparation in resource center
8:45-10:25	Teaching reading to students from grades one through three in resource center
10:25-10:35	Break
10:35-11:20	Team teaching math to third grade students in regular classroom
11:20-12:00	Lunch
12:00-1:00	Individual tutoring/preparation in resource center

1:00-1:45	Team teaching math to second grade students in regular classroom
1:45-2:00	Individual tutoring in resource center
2:00-3:45	Preparation/conferences

Assistance from the communication disorders specialist and the school psychologist is also a reasonable expectation. Integrating handicapped children into the regular classroom and effectively educating them is neither simple nor inexpensive. There is a danger that school administrators may perceive the integration of the mildly handicapped child into the regular classroom as an economy measure. Regular educators must be aware of state regulations governing funding and guidelines for programs for the handicapped so they may fully realize the level of assistance they have a right to expect.

THE "UNLABELED" CHILD

Many elementary and intermediate classrooms contain handicapped children who are not labeled. Teachers sometimes fear that referring a child for clinical assessment will stigmatize and ultimately ostracize the child and many even reflect badly on themselves. There is no empirical basis for such fears, and the failure to refer handicapped children serves primarily to deprive them of additional educational services that could significantly accelerate their school performance. (For a thorough discussion of this subject, see the *American Journal of Mental Deficiency*, November, 1974, *79*, no. 3 pp. 241-73.) To assist the teacher in making necessary referrals for clinical assessment, the following three sections describe the most common handicapping conditions.

Mildly Mentally Retarded Children

According to the widely accepted definition of the American Association on Mental Deficiency, "Mental retardation refers to significantly subaverage intellectual functioning existing concurrently with deficits in adaptive behavior manifested during the developmental period" (Grossman, 1973, p. 5). Though frequently criticized, an individually administered test to determine the intelligence quotient (IQ) remains the soundest clinical tool in determining the level of intellectual functioning. Currently children with IQs ranging from 55 to 69 are considered mildly or educable mentally retarded, and these children are often mainstreamed (see Figure 1.1).

It is important to remember that, generally speaking, IQ scores are dispersed across the normal curve and that being mentally retarded means that one's IQ falls close to the tail of the curve (see Figure 1.2). The normal curve indicates that there are many more "average" people than there are gifted or retarded individuals. Because intelligence is on a continuum, students with a 75 IQ may share many of the learning problems of children with an IQ of 69, though they may or may not be considered eligible for special education services.

At this point the qualifying statements in the definition of mental retardation are revelant. The regular educator should be particularly cognizant of "deficits in adaptive behavior manifested during the developmental period." Many states are

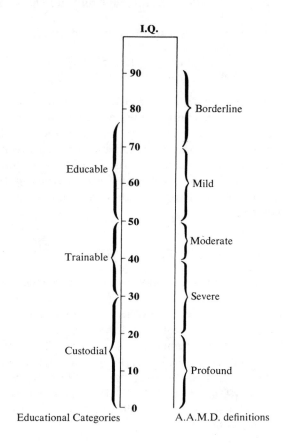

FIGURE 1.1 *Classification Systems for the Mentally Retarded*

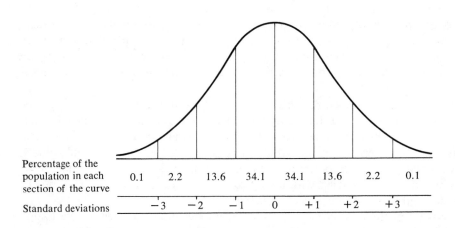

FIGURE 1.2. *Theoretical Normal Probability Curve of Intelligence*

considering other variables in addition to IQ scores to determine if a student is eligible for special education services. Deficits in the academic, physical, and social functioning of the child are considered. The arbitrary use of a single IQ score which is precisely two standard deviations from normal as a cut off in determining eligibility is now usually replaced by a range of scores. Decisions regarding eligibility for services are made after consulting these scores, which reflect the handicapped student's behavioral deficits.

A child should be considered for referral if the teacher observes the following:

1. Development is obviously delayed. The child is smaller than other children in stature. Coordination is poor compared to that of age mates. Babyish or inappropriate social behavior is frequent.
2. The child is significantly behind his age mates in academic acquisition. He works slowly and shows little evidence of being able to generalize what he learns.
3. The family is poor. The vast majority of mildly mentally retarded individuals come from low socioeconomic stratas of society, where lack of early stimulation sometimes produces the "six-hour retarded child," who is academically retarded compared to his middle class age mates. (McCandless, 1964, pp. 192-93)

The presence of a mentally retarded child in the typical middle-class regular classroom is invariably and dramatically apparent. These children "significantly differ" from their peers in the areas outlined by McCandless and should be referred for clinical assessment. On the other hand, the classroom that served predominantly lower-class children presents a more difficult problem of discriminating "significant" deficits. Teachers should consider the following question: Is the present level of educational service failing to improve the functioning of the child? If so, even if a considerable number of children in the class meet this criterion, referrals should be made to offer the best hope of providing additional resources through special education services.

Learning and Language Disabled

We are much better at describing what "learning and language disabled" isn't than what it is. It is not mental retardation. It is not emotional disturbance, though children labeled as learning and language disabled frequently develop some symptoms of emotional disturbance. It is not the result of a sensory handicap. Many experts postulate minimal brain dysfunction as the cause of L/LDs (learning/language disabilities), but this idea has not aided educators in the task of assessment and classification. The etiological mystery itself confounds teachers and bewilders parents.

The handicap known as learning and language disability is characterized by the discrepancy between expectation and reality. Most children with this handicap perform academically at a level significantly below their peers even though they have normal, above normal, or slightly below normal IQs. In the folklore of special education it is common to see listed a number of symptoms such children may or may not have, including hyperactivity, short attention span, impulsivity, emotional lability, and perceptual-motor impairment (McCarthy & McCarthy, 1969, p. 8). However, none of these symptoms has proved to be universal across this population. The only universal characteristic is significantly reduced performance in reading, spoken language, writing, and/or mathematics skills.

This deficit is not of the remedial type that shows quick improvement when the teacher gives extra help. It is a pervasive disability that demands highly structured, individualized instruction. Hyperactivity and other symptoms, though frequently mentioned in the literature, may be the *effects* of dramatic school failure rather than the cause.

Most states provide special education funding for children with learning disabilities. It is generally agreed that approximately 3% of school population children have learning disabilities severe enough to need special education services. An additional 17% will need special help within the regular classroom (Washington State Special Education Commission, 1974). More and more special educators are being prepared to work effectively with these children, and the regular teacher should call on them for assistance in preparing the pupils' educational programs. The most successful techniques for instructing handicapped children are invariably delivered on an individual or small group basis and may be physically beyond the reach of a teacher with a class of thirty.

The vast majority of children with learning and language disabilities are boys, and their families are predominantly middle-class. It is sometimes hypothesized that many of these children's learning problems are the result of poor instruction in the early elementary grades. Whatever the cause, many are not diagnosed until the fourth grade or later. By that time the problem has begun to be a highly charged emotional issue within the family.

The child who is not acquiring academic skills should be referred for clinical assessment as early as possible to reduce the obvious consequences of repeated failure. Parents are frequently victimized by promises of quick cures. Drugs have been used effectively to control "symptoms" such as hyperactivity, but sometimes the child is sedated to the point where learning is further impaired. Although perceptual-motor activities have been advocated, subsequent research has not supported their efficacy (Hallahan & Cruickshank, 1973).

Emotional Disturbance

Emotional disturbance (or behavior disability) is a condition that is difficult to describe. Most teachers would feel comfortable with their ability to recognize severe emotional disturbance; many movies, television, and popular magazines portray various types of severe disturbance with surprising regularity. However, since such children are usually referred to outside agencies, the regular classroom teacher rarely encounters severely disturbed children in the classroom. What is required of a teacher is to be able to spot such children and refer them to the proper agencies for help.

Mild emotional disturbance is a more difficult syndrome to define and tends to be situational to some degree. While teachers tend to be intolerant of variations in what they personally consider acceptable social behavior, there is great variation in the amount and degree of deviant social behavior that will be accepted. Families also share this kind of variability in tolerance. For example, in some situations deficits in listening to and following directions, lack of motivation to learn, occasional temper tantrums, impudence, and swearing may be considered causes for referral for psychological and/or medical help. In other educational settings all of these behaviors may be considered normal because they are widely shared by the reference group.

Educators should use as a rule of thumb in making referrals the degree to which a child's behavior interferes with his classmates' or his own acquisition of school learning. Chapter 4 discusses techniques that can be used with individuals or groups of children to modify unacceptable classroom behavior. These management techniques should be tried before children are referred for special treatment. However, before teachers exhaust their entire repertoire of management methods, help should be requested. Help does not necessarily mean that the child will be removed from the class if found eligible for special education services. More likely it means that additional resources will be allocated to provide help for the mildly emotionally disturbed child *remaining* in the regular classroom.

Many teachers confuse emotional disturbance and juvenile delinquency. Although many juvenile delinquents are emotionally disturbed, not all emotionally disturbed children are delinquent. Delinquency has to do with breaking the law and getting caught. Some delinquents possess excellent school records but exhibit deviant behavior in other situations. The ecological model of emotional disturbance suggests that the problem of emotional disturbance does not lie in the child or in the environment but rather in the interaction of the two. Juvenile delinquency is just one possible response to that impaired interaction. Juvenile delinquents, unless they are judged seriously emotionally disturbed, are not eligible for services under P.L. 94-142.

In the past special education has often served as a "holding pen" for emotionally disturbed children. Many special classes composed entirely of emotionally disturbed children degenerated rapidly into custodial placement with little evident progress in school learning or improved behavioral change. Few teachers faced with homogeneously grouped emotionally disturbed children are able to cope for more than two or three years regardless of their preparation. Behavioral specialists are being trained to assist the regular teacher in programming for emotionally disturbed children in the mainstream of education. Only the most severe cases should be removed from the regular class, and only the children who are a physical danger to themselves and others should be removed from the school program.

Treatments for the behaviorally disordered child will be dealt with in Chapter 4. Generally these treatments involve both the modification of behaviors that interfere with school learning and the modification of the school environment. Emotionally disturbed children respond favorably to stable, predictable environments. Therefore, the careful structuring of the school program is essential. Often contingency management is effective in increasing motivation and consequently in improving acquisition. Drug therapy is sometimes recommended for the behaviorally disordered as it is for children with learning and language disabilities. In fact, the overlap between these two categories is considerable. However, the behavior of emotionally disturbed children is of more concern to parents and professionals than is that of children who exhibit deficits in school learning.

Again, boys are most frequently referred as emotionally disturbed and found eligible for special education service. Incidence depends upon the many situational variables discussed above and may range from 2% to 10% of the school population (Hewitt, 1968, p. 4). Children from lower socio-economic families are most frequently represented (Graubard, 1973, pp. 254-55).

Regular elementary or intermediate teachers attempting to integrate and educate exceptional children in their classrooms will need to learn special education methods. These are methods that will probably benefit nonhandicapped children in the classroom as well. Proficiency in individualizing instruction, behavior modification, adaptation of materials, and the efficient use of assistance from the special educator, the communication disorders specialist, and the school psychologist will be essential for successfully integrating and educating the mildly handicapped child in the regular classroom.

2

Least Restrictive Environment

THE CONCEPTS

With the passage of Public Law 94–142, "The Education For All Handicapped Children Act," and the implementation of Section 504 of the Vocational Rehabilitation Act of 1973, local control of educational decision making regarding the placement of handicapped students in the schools was significantly altered. While the federal legislation imposes constraints on the schools regarding placement because they can no longer make these decisions alone, it also distributes responsibility for making those decisions to include the parents. We would describe P.L. 94–142 as a conservative law because it returns power to parents concerning the education of their children. P.L. 94–142 requires that each state must submit a plan that includes means for meeting the least restrictive environment provision, which requires that each state must establish:

> . . . procedures to assure that, to the maximum extent appropriate, handicapped children, including children in public or private institutions or other care facilities, are educated with children who are not handicapped, and that special classes, separate schooling, or other removal of handicapped children from the regular educational environment occurs only when the nature and severity of the handicap is such that education in regular classes with the use of supplementary aids and services cannot be achieved satisfactorily. (Sec. 612 (5))

James Q. Affleck and Sheila Lowenbraun

15

The language and intent are very clear to us: the burden of proof rests with the school to justify why any child is *not* placed in regular classes. Therefore, the schools must be able to present placement options at the Individualized Education Program (IEP) conference (which is also mandated by P.L. 94–142) and negotiate a plan with the parent or guardian, keeping in mind that the least restrictive alternative must be selected.

> The crux of the solution is that the planning of delivery systems must create one integrated system of alternatives open to all children, not one for the so-called normals and another for the handicapped. There must be one system which is and remains basic for all children and serves as the function for bringing to handicapped children the services they need. (Abeson, 1976, p. 520)

The parallels with racial desegregation findings (*Brown* v. *Board of Education,* 1954) are striking. The practice of having separate but equal facilities is replaced by the concept that all separate facilities are "inherently unequal."

Though Section 504 of the Vocational Rehabilitation Act of 1973 is very similar to P.L. 94–142 in regard to least restrictive environment (LRE) provisions, additional requirements are made. Section 84.34 of Subpart D of the new law specifies that each handicapped person shall be educated with nonhandicapped persons to the maximum extent possible to meet his or her educational needs. If an alternative placement is deemed necessary because of the nature and severity of a person's handicap, proximity to the person's home must be considered. Nonacademic and extracurricular services must also be provided with nonhandicapped persons.

Again the burden of proof rests with the schools to justify why the handicapped student is not in the regular classroom in his neighborhood school, fully participating in nonacademic and extracurricular activities.

Compliance

The citations above are included to emphasize how the federal mandate contrasts with past educational practice. Federal compliance auditing is taking place and the LRE provisions are attended to with increasing rigor. Failure to meet these and other provisions can lead to sanctions resulting in the loss of federal funds for an entire state. Yet even if a state chooses not to receive federal funds, it must still comply with the law because of the binding provisions of Section 504 of the Vocational Rehabilitation Act of 1973. The Commissioner of Education is directed by the law to review and monitor state plans and to regulate them through monitoring, auditing, and sanction procedures. (For an overview of the functions of the federal, state, and local governments concerning the implementation of P.L. 94–142, see Table 2.1.)

To many educators, including school board members and chief state school officers, this new law enforcement system has emerged with dismaying speed and force. Complaints regarding over-regulation, erosion of local control of the schools, and federal insensitivity to local and state educational problems have been duly registered. This opposition may effectively lead to amendment of some provisions of the law. However, we feel that the LRE mandate will not and cannot be substantially changed.

TABLE 2.1

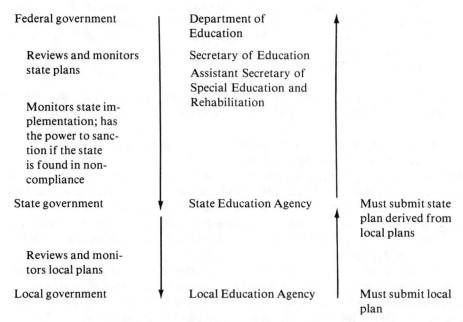

Federal government	Department of Education	
Reviews and monitors state plans	Secretary of Education	
	Assistant Secretary of Special Education and Rehabilitation	
Monitors state implementation; has the power to sanction if the state is found in noncompliance		
State government	State Education Agency	Must submit state plan derived from local plans
Reviews and monitors local plans		
Local government	Local Education Agency	Must submit local plan

Origins and Support for Least Restrictive Environment In Legal Precedent

As Lowenbraun and Affleck (1978) note in a discussion of the Least Restrictive Environment prepared for the Bureau of Education for the Handicapped, the least restrictive alternative principle arose out of the due process clause of the 14th Amendment to the U.S. Constitution. Although many court cases have been based upon the principle that all children have a right to a free appropriate public education, the courts have also addressed the issue of appropriateness of educational programs in a manner that relates directly to the least restrictive environment concept:

> Prior to the 1960's, handicapped children were often excluded from the public schools or placed in substandard educational settings without any hearing regarding placement. Consequently, the doctrines of due process and the least restrictive alternative emerged as the legal principles upon which much of the litigation in special education has been based. This litigation in turn has resulted in the incorporation of due process and least restrictive alternative provisions in both state and federal legislation culminating in the enactment of P.L. 94-142. (Chiba & Semmel, 1977, p. 19)

Two court cases that specifically related to the requirements of the least restrictive environment were the *Pennsylvania Association for Retarded Children* v. *Commonwealth of Pennsylvania* (*PARC,* 1971) and *Mills* v. *Board of Education of the District of Columbia* (*Mills,* 1972). In the former case, the court ruled that:

> It is the Commonwealth's obligation to place each mentally retarded child in a free, public program of education and training appropriate to the child's capacity, within the context of a presumption that, among the alternative programs of education and training required by statute to be available, placement in a regular public school class is preferable . . . to placement in any other type of program of education. (334 FSupp. at 1260)

The *Mills* case ordered the implementation of due process and least restrictive alternatives not only for mentally retarded children, but also for *all* handicapped children.

Other kinds of litigation have extended the areas of concern. In a class action suit, *Diana* v. *Board of Education* (Diana, 1970), nine Mexican-American children alleged that they had been placed inappropriately in a class for the mentally retarded on the basis of inaccurate test scores. This suit led, among other due process safeguards, to a provisioin in the California code that "children of any ethnic, socio-economic, and cultural group not be placed in classes or special programs for the educable mentally retarded if they can be served in regular classes" (Chiba & Semmel, 1977, p. 20).

In the *Wyatt* v. *Stickney* (1972) decision, the judge ruled, concerning Partlow State School, that "no person shall be admitted to the institution unless a prior determination shall have been made that residence in the institution is the least restrictive habilitation setting feasible for that person" (Soskin, 1977, p. 29).

In the Willowbrook case *(New York State Association for Retarded Children* v. *Carey),* the court ordered that the population of the Willowbrook State School of 5700 residents be reduced to 250 or fewer within six years. In a similar case, *Horacek* v. *Exon* (1975), the population of Beatrice State School was to be decreased from 1000 to 250 within three years (Soskin, 1977, p. 28-32).

There have also been recent attempts within the state courts to mandate placement of mentally retarded persons in less restrictive environments within the community. In the case of *Joyce Z.* (1975), the judge ruled that a profoundly retarded girl be placed with foster parents in the community rather than in an institution and that the state pay for this special foster home. In the case of *Stephanie L.* (1977), the court ruled that this 17-year-old mildly retarded girl no longer required institutionalization, but that she did need a "closely supervised, structured residential program in her own community which could provide essential behavior modification programs to help her adjust to living in the community" (Soskin, 1977, p. 32). The judge ruled that this placement be organized and funded.

Many federal and state court cases have created or upheld the principle of the least restrictive alternative for placement of handicapped individuals. These court cases, together with federal and state laws, culminated in the enactment of P.L. 94-142. Undoubtedly, this principle will need to be defended many more times in our nation's courts before total implementation is realized. However, the foundation for ensuring this basic right of handicapped children to be educated in the least restrictive environment has been well established and will continue to be built upon (Lowenbraun and Affleck, 1978).

Summary

Having analyzed the laws, rules and regulations, and jurisprudence, we have deduced the following general guidelines concerning LRE.

1. All handicapped children have the right to an education in the least restrictive environment possible for them.
2. Placement in a less restrictive environment cannot be denied simply because the option does not exist in a specific service district. If an option does not exist, but is deemed appropriate for a given child, legal precedent mandates the establishing and funding of the appropriate placement.
3. A child's placement is determined after, and because of, the Individualized Education Program Conference. No child may be placed in an educational environment simply on the basis of a categorical label or presumed level of functioning.
4. The least restrictive environment concept is not synonymous with the concept of mainstreaming. LRE mandates a continuum of services; mainstreaming is one point along that continuum. (Lowenbraun & Affleck, 1978, p.23)

COPING WITH THE LEAST RESTRICTIVE ENVIRONMENT

Given the inevitability of implementing the LRE provisions, regular education teachers need to take the following steps to make accommodations within the law so that quality education for all children is not sacrificed.

As a regular elementary teacher, you will find it useful to:

1. Read the law and rules and regulations for P.L. 94-142 and Section 504 of the Vocational Rehabilitation Act. For instance, subsection 84.34 of Section 504 provides that if a handicapped child's behavior is so disruptive in a regular classroom as to seriously impair the learning of the other children, such placement may be determined to be inappropriate. (For a review of the major procedures set forth in P.L. 94-142, see chapter 3.)

2. Read your school district's plan for implementation, paying particular attention to the allocation of resources that accompany the placement of a handicapped student. Remember that relatively large sums of money have been allocated to ensure a free appropriate educational program in the least restrictive environment. Therefore, placing a handicapped student in your classroom without compensatory service to you and the student should immediately be questioned.

3. Read the Individualized Education Programs for each child. This will provide you with further information regarding the school district's agreements with parents or guardians regarding compensatory services for the handicapped students in your class.

4. If your school district has a teachers' union or organization, read the negotiated agreement of your school district and the collective bargaining

agent. This might, for example, permit you to know such things as the district's policy on drug administration and other health service obligations that may be expected of you as a classroom teacher. Knowing your rights and responsibilities in these areas may protect you from a malpractice action. Further, the agreement may disclose your rights to further training at school district, state, or federal expense.

5. Work closely with parents. After initial placement, many parents of handicapped students may want to communicate with the professionals who are directly instructing their children. Later in this book you will find a system for reporting a child's progress. Many parents of handicapped children have become sophisticated in expecting objective data rather than impressionistic reporting of their child's achievement. By law, you will be expected to work toward implementing educational objectives that the parents and school district have previously determined. Reporting to the parents regarding the child's learning *related to those objectives* puts your relationship to them on a proper professional and legal level.

6. Approach these changes with the attitude that they offer a challenge rather than an additional burden. If you follow these suggestions, you will find that although you have to individualize more of your program, you will have more assistance; if you have to keep more data on child progress, you will know more about your effectiveness as a teacher; and if you have to work more closely with parents, there is more opportunity for important school learning to be enhanced and extended at home.

7. Become familiar with the due process provisions for parents and staff outlined in P.L. 94-142, Rules and Regulations.

There is no doubt that implementation of the new laws will change the role of the teacher. The increased responsibilities of the elementary teacher will be demanding, and challenging, with new opportunities to show leadership and organizational ability.

3

Systematic Instruction and The Effect of P.L. 94–142

As a regular classroom teacher, you will find children in your classroom who differ substantially from the other children. These children may be academically deficient; they may not learn as quickly as others; they may need special adaptations of instructional tasks because of sensory or physical handicaps; or they may exhibit behavior that is disruptive or unacceptable in the classroom. But no matter what the composition of your class, you are responsible for academic growth in *all* children, including those who are "educationally different." While all children benefit from an educational approach that recognizes their special needs, educationally different children need specially designed programs of direct and systematic instruction in order to maximize their growth.

The following chapters discuss the various components of a systematic instructional model (see Table 3.1) which are crucial for instructing mildly handicapped children.

Mildly handicapped refers to handicapping conditions of relative severity that do not preclude partial or full time placement in the regular classroom. Generally, mildly handicapped children have been classified as mildly retarded, learning disabled, or behaviorally disordered.

THE INSTRUCTIONAL MODEL

The model begins with initial assessment, that of collecting information on the child's current functioning level in academic and nonacademic areas. The assess-

Anita Archer

ment information is used to establish annual goals and short-term objectives (sequential steps leading to the annual goals). Instructional activities, including direct teacher instruction and practice, are then selected to match the short-term objectives. At this time, a data recording system is planned to regularly monitor the mastery of the objectives. Once an instructional plan is implemented, the classroom teacher can decide, on the basis of data collected through ongoing assessment, whether modification of instructional activities is necessary.

TABLE 3.1
Systematic Instructional Model

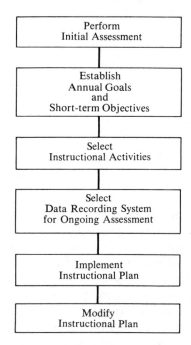

This general model of instruction is appropriate in all teaching situations in the elementary school. However, a more precise application is necessary when one works with "educationally different" children. Educationally different children include those who have been identified and classified as mildly handicapped for whom total or partial placement in the regular classroom has been determined as the least restrictive environment. This model of instruction is equally applicable to nonhandicapped, low-performing children who do not readily retain new information and are easily confused during instruction. Using direct and systematic instruction in the basic skill areas (e.g., reading, spelling, math, written expression, and handwriting) is particularly critical when a child is having a great deal of difficulty or is performing below the classroom norm. If the child is handicapped, the areas of special need will be outlined in his IEP.

Though direct and systematic instruction is critical to the mildly handicapped child, its implementation is not solely the responsibility of the regular classroom teacher. Some mildly handicapped children placed in a regular classroom may require additional instruction or services which cannot be provided in the regular classroom. Special education personnel often provide services to these handicapped students or to the regular classroom teacher within the regular classroom. In other cases, they may instruct the students in a resource room outside of the regular classroom for relatively short periods of time. Resource room personnel generally provide very systematic instruction in basic skill areas using individual or small-group instruction. Additional personnel such as remedial reading teachers, communication disorders specialists (speech therapists), and Title I teachers are often available to serve handicapped children as well as nonhandicapped, low-performing children.

Another procedure for instructing educationally different children is regrouping for basic skill instruction across grade levels or within a grade level. Children with similar needs can thus be served by one teacher, increasing the efficiency of instruction.

You should seek appropriate help from other professionals whenever possible. This can save you from duplicating efforts and enable our schools to provide maximum services to the largest number of children. Though you should vigorously seek special services for children in your classroom, you will still be responsible for systematically teaching the educationally different students in academic areas in which special services are not provided. You will also be responsible for reinforcing skills taught outside of your classroom and accommodating the child's participation in classroom activities that overlap with external services. For example, though the child may receive spelling assistance in the resource room, he still will need spelling assistance when completing classroom written reports. Likewise, the student who attends the resource room or remedial reading classroom for daily reading instruction will still require help with reading in the regular classroom (e.g., assistance in selecting appropriate books for independent reading, alternative reading materials for social studies, practice exercises to complete during the reading period when the child is in the classroom). The provision of educational services to the mildly handicapped child thus becomes a cooperative effort with the regular classroom teacher a critical member of the instructional team.

A certain mystique surrounding the education of mildly handicapped children has often convinced regular classroom teachers that teaching these children is substantially different from teaching most children in the regular classroom. Certainly there are some differences. The sequential steps of instruction often need to be smaller, the instruction more precise, the practice more carefully designed, the number of repetitions during instruction and practice increased, and children's progress measured more often. However, the similarities are more important. Like the regular classroom student, the handicapped child needs to learn basic academic skills, to be taught at his or her level of performance, to be directly taught new skills, to practice new skills to mastery. As a regular classroom teacher, you do not need a whole new repertoire of teaching skills for mildly handicapped students or a totally divergent type of instructional program. Instead, you will need to apply your existing skills in a more precise, systematic fashion.

PROCEDURES OUTLINED IN P.L. 94–142

Though instructional models such as the systematic instruction we suggest in this book have long been used by many special educators, P.L. 94-142, through its provisions and accompanying rules and regulations, has made this model of instruction standard procedure when working with handicapped children. Before describing specific components of the systematic instructional model, we will review the major procedures set forth in P.L. 94–142 and their effect on the education of handicapped children and on the regular classroom teachers serving them.

Special Services Committee

Within each school, a permanent committee, often called the special services committee, coordinates and monitors all activities in identifying, evaluating, and placing handicapped children within special education and related services. The permanent members of this committee include individuals responsible for providing special education services such as the special education teacher(s), the resource room teacher(s), the school counselor, the school psychologist, and the principal or vice principal. When the committee is considering a specific child, additional members may be added because of their relationship to the child (e.g., the regular classroom teacher who has referred the child to the special services committee for evaluation) or their expertise regarding the child's suspected handicapping condition (e.g., the speech therapist if the child is referred because of a suspected communication disorder). This permanent committee plays a critical role in all activities related to special education including referral, evaluation, and development, implementation, and progress review of IEPs. However, many of the specific responsibilities are assigned to other committees (e.g., multidisciplinary evaluation teams, IEP committees) or individuals (e.g., implementors of IEPs).

Referral

A referral is a formal written request made to the special services committee for an evaluation of the special needs of a child who has become a "focus of concern" because of poor academic performance, behavior problems in school or at home, or possible physical handicaps such as visual problems. Professional members of the school staff, particularly regular classroom teachers, identify these children who may need special services, determine if there is adequate information on which to base the referral, and actually write the referral and submit it to the special services committee. Since referral is the initial step in providing special education and related services, it is critical in providing appropriate education to handicapped children.

Though referral procedures and referral forms differ among school districts, the referring agent, often the regular classroom teacher, is generally asked to specify the *nature of the school-related problems,* as well as any *formal or informal information* that has been utilized to substantiate the concerns. Areas of functioning in which problems could occur include academic achievement, intellectual functioning, social-emotional behaviors, motor skills, language and communication skills, speech, hearing, and vision. Within each of these areas, the referring agent then describes the nature of the problem. For example, the teacher might make the following notations on the referral form:

Academic achievement:

> Functions substantially below third grade level in math.
> Has difficulty with simple addition and subtraction.

Social-emotional behavior:

> Continually talks out in class. Doesn't stay in his seat during independent work sessions. Disturbs other children. Engages in fights at recess.

Language and communication skills:

> Cannot follow two-step directions given in class.
> Has difficulty expressing common experiences verbally.
> For example, cannot describe an event during show and tell.

It is also helpful if the referring agent describes informal information (e.g., observations made of the child, discussions with other professionals, conferences with parents) and formal information (e.g., achievement test scores, assessment information collected within the classroom, results of vision tests, previous grades, records of classroom behavior) that substantiate the concern. When the problem is clearly stated and the formal and informal information is collected, the special services committee can proceed with formal evaluation of the child.

Evaluation

A child is required to have a full, individual assessment prior to placement in special education. This assessment has two purposes: (a) to determine if the child is eligible for special education services because a handicap necessitates specially designed instruction and (b) the nature and extent of special education and related services that the child requires. As a result, the formal evaluation involves categorizing as well as program planning.

Upon receipt of the referral, the special services committee writes a letter to and possibly has a conference with the parents to request consent to evaluate their child. The letter to the parents should describe the action proposed by the school, in this case full evaluation of their child to determine educational needs and possible eligibility for special education. The letter must also describe the nature of the tests to be administered, what would happen to the child depending on the outcome of the evaluation, and a listing of their parental rights. When the parents have given consent for the formal evaluation, the special services committee assigns a multidisciplinary evaluation team to evaluate the child. The multidisciplinary team must include at least one teacher or other specialist who has knowledge of the suspected handicapping condition.

The rules and regulations govern the selection and administration of assessment tools. The child is to be assessed in all areas related to the suspected disability (e.g., health, vision, social and emotional behaviors, general intelligence, motor abilities, communication skills, and academic performance) using tests that are tailored to measure specific areas of need as well as those tests which measure a single general intelligence quotient. The tests used must be validated for the specific purpose for which they are chosen. For example, if the purpose is to determine eligibility, the test must be designed to determine a handicapping condition. If the test results are to be used in program planning, it must be valid for that purpose. The rules and regulations also require that the evaluation be non-discriminatory and that bias be reduced by testing the child in his or her native language and considering socio-cultural factors in reviewing the evaluation information. Generally, norm-referenced tests will be used to determine if the child meets the state and federal guidelines for eligibility for special education, but information, such as observations of the child, can be used to confirm the findings. A broader range of tests can be used to determine current functioning levels, the basis on which the goals and objectives are established for the child. These procedures may include norm-referenced diagnostic tests, criterion-referenced tests, informal assessment tools, and classroom observation. Assessment procedures for determining a child's current functioning level as a basis of the individual education program are explained more completely in Chapter 5.

After collecting the evaluation data, each team member writes a formal report on the child. The team then reviews all of the information, determines if the child is eligible for special education or related services, and contacts the parents to explain the evaluation results. Within that letter or at a parallel conference, the process for developing an individualized education program for their child is introduced and their parental rights are again outlined.

Individualized Education Programs

If a child in your classroom has been determined eligible for special education or related services because of physical, hearing, vision or speech impairments, or because of mental retardation, learning disabilities, behavior disorders, or a combination of these handicapping conditions, an Individualized Education Program (IEP) will be formulated for the child. At the core of the IEP are the three components of systematic instruction that we have discussed: a description of the child's current functioning level in those areas in which special education or related services are required; long-term goals that seem reasonable for the child to meet by the end of the school year; and the short-term objectives (sequential steps) that will lead to attainment of those goals. In addition to current functioning level, goals, and objectives, the written document states the services needed by the child to meet the goals and objectives, the professional or instructional staff members who will be responsible for delivering those services, the degree and nature of the child's placement in the regular classroom, and the evaluation procedures that will be used at least on an annual basis to measure the child's progress toward the stated goals and objectives so that the IEP can be altered and updated.

The IEP is prepared for the child by the regular classroom and special education teachers serving the handicapped child, a designated representative of the school district such as the director of special education, the principal or school psychologist, and the parent(s) or guardian(s) of the handicapped child. The child is also encouraged to participate in the preparation of the IEP if possible. All persons who participate in the meeting must agree with the objectives and procedures formulated in the plan, which is usually formalized by signing the IEP.

Each person participating in planning the IEP contributes information concerning the child's current educational functioning level which should have direct relevance to planning an instructional program that includes objectives and possible interventions. Specific medical or psychological findings will not be presented unless directly translatable into educational interventions. Participants may share any information that will be helpful in planning for the child.

Any of the procedures discussed in Chapter 3 can be used to collect relevant information to establish current functioning level. For example, the reading teacher might present information on general and specific reading skills as determined from a number of commercially prepared diagnostic tests. The classroom teacher might supply additional information on reading performance from informal reading inventories used to place the child in a basal reader, from an informal sequence-based survey of the child's decoding skills, and from a test of irregular word recognition. In addition, the classroom teacher may share review assignments from classroom materials that have been completed by the child. The parents are also encouraged to bring information on the child's current functioning level. For example, they might bring prior report cards, work from the prior year, or any testing information collected outside of the school that would contribute to program planning.

In preparing for the IEP meeting, participants should not only collect and summarize information on current functioning level, but they should also determine potential areas that might require special service programming. Written drafts of portions of the IEP, especially the long-term goals and short-term objectives, may be outlined before the meeting. While the process of participatory planning and collecting information from all parties should not be circumvented by the signing of a pre-written document, we recommend prior preparation of portions of the IEP. It is important that any prepared drafts be presented only as proposals on which additional input and modifications will be accepted.

Though the actual process used in the meeting varies from district to district, the following outline has proven effective. To begin, the chairperson introduces participants, reviews the purpose of the meeting, outlines the procedures to be followed, and makes arrangements for recording the proceedings. The first step is presentation and review of the child's current functioning level. It is often helpful at this point to identify areas of special concern for the child (e.g., reading, spelling, math, behavior problems), and to report current functioning level in each of these areas. After the current functioning level has been summarized in each area deemed critical to the handicapped child, long-term goals are determined.

The listing of short-term objectives may include all sequential steps leading to mastery of the long-term goal or be limited to major milestones. The short-term objectives must be measurable and be stated in behavioral terms. As noted earlier in this chapter, both the extraction of sequences from commercial materials and the independent writing of sequences is a lengthy process and not easily accomplished in the IEP meeting. For this reason, instructional sequences in probable areas of special need should be written prior to the IEP meeting. Alternatively, the committee should choose to write only major milestones for each long-term objective with the responsibility for further breakdown going to the designated implementor of the program.

If instruction related to a goal can be implemented in the regular class when special services are provided, the regular classroom teacher may be designated as the implementor. For other goals, support staff including special education teachers, resource room teachers, remedial teachers, speech therapists, or counselors may be given responsibility for implementation.

Though the written document will vary a great deal from district to district, the components will be constant. A portion of the IEP written for Molly is shown in Table 3.2.

TABLE 3.2

A portion of the IEP written for Molly

NAME _Molly Davis_   SEX _Female_   GRADE _6th_   DATE OF BIRTH _4/5/66_   C.A. _12_

ADDRESS _1700 Green Street_   TELEPHONE NUMBER _345-8970_

PARENT(s), GUARDIAN(s), SURROGATE _Tom and Louise Davis_

Date of the IEP meeting(s) _Initial meeting 9/9/78 Final meeting 9/10/78_

	TEAM MEMBER	POSITION	SIGNATURE
Chairperson	Kate Turner	Director, Special Education	
	Dennis Fredericks	6th grade teacher	
	Mary Grace	Resource Room Teacher	
	Ann Ross	Reading Teacher	
	Tom Davis	Father	
	Louis Davis	Mother	

Present placement of child _Regular class + Resource Room_   Recommendation for placement _Regular class + Resource room_

Percentage of time in the regular education program _66%_

Justification for placement: _Molly should be in the resource room for at least one hour of instruction in reading and language arts. She should receive addition 45 minutes minutes of instruction in math in the resource room. All additional services should be carried out in the regular classroom including special instruction in spelling._ Date of program entry _9-15-78_ Anticipated duration of special education or related services _9-78 to 6-79_ Summary of special education and related services needed: _Resource room-special education services. Materials- no special materials except a programmed math book for practice in the regular class. Related services - none._

TABLE 3.2-(con't)

A portion of the IEP written for Molly

Area of instruction ___MATH___

Summary of Current functioning level: <u>Facts</u>: On timed probes, Molly could quickly compute addition facts to 5 and subtraction facts with minuends to 5. However, she was very slow and inaccurate on more difficult facts. She has no knowledge of x facts. <u>Operations</u>: On both the KEYMATH test and informal tests, Molly could perform + and - operations involving no regrouping. <u>Money</u>: Can name and tell value of coins. <u>Time</u>: Can tell time to hour and half hours. <u>Fractions</u>: no skills.

Long Term Goals	Short term objectives Major milestones (★ See attached sequences)	Services needed to meet goals/objectives	Annual Review
Will solve addition and subtraction facts.	When given a sheet of + facts with sums to 10, will write answer with 40 per minute and no more than one error.	Resource Room— Mary Beth Goodwin	
	When given a sheet of + facts with sums to 18, Molly will write answers with 40 per minute and no more than one error.		
	When given a sheet of subtraction facts with minuends to 10, Molly will write answers with 40 per minute and no more than one error.		
	When given a sheet of subtraction facts with minuends to 18, Molly will write answers with 40 per minute and no more than 1 error.		
Will solve additional computations involving 3 digit plus 3 digit with regrouping.	When given 20 problems, 2 dig. + 1 dig. with regrouping, Molly will write answers with 95% accuracy.	Resource Room— Mary Beth Goodwin	
	When given 20 problems, 2 dig. + 2 dig. with regrouping, Molly will write answers with 95% accuracy.	Additional practice using Sullivan Programmed Math Books in Regular Class-	
	When given 20 problems, 3 dig. + 3 dig. with regrouping, Molly will write answers with 95% accuracy.	Dennis Archey	
	(More complete sequence attached.)		

Procedures for evaluating progress toward long term goals:

Facts: Daily timings will be taken on facts with daily performance graphed. A post test will be given on all additional and subtraction facts.

Addition Operations: Daily probes will be taken on addition computations.

Responsibilities of the Regular Classroom Teacher in the IEP process.

As a regular classroom teacher serving children who have been classified as handicapped, you will take an active and vital role in writing and carrying out the child's IEP. You will need to (1) collect information on the child's current functioning level through formal and informal assessment procedures and direct observation in the classroom; (2) determine what skills (long-term goals) the child needs to be taught; (3) write instructional sequences generally extracted from commercial materials available in your classroom or building and, when designated, in the IEP; (4) implement instruction based on the long-term goals.

Because the IEP is not a legally binding document, regular classroom teachers are not held accountable for meeting each of the long-term goals specified in the IEP. But although the IEP is only a planning document designed to assist professionals in serving handicapped children, you *are* responsible for providing quality instruction, for making a good faith effort at meeting the instructional objectives, and for using a "reasonable standard" of instruction when working with the handicapped child. When you use direct and systematic instructional procedures, the handicapped child may indeed achieve. However, a number of factors may interfere with the child's mastery of long-term goals. For example, the goals may have been set beyond the child's reach; the child may have been absent a great deal during the year; or the best instructional interventions for the child may not have been determined soon enough. Keep in mind that the goals and objectives are a projection for the child, a direction toward which instruction should move. However, the success of the IEP should be judged on the progress made and quality of efforts made at reaching the long-term goals rather than attainment of all of the objectives. If absolute accountability for meeting the goals were required, the goals would often be set too low, thus lowering expectations for the handicapped child and not providing enough direction for classroom teachers.

4

Classroom Management

One of the main problems faced by all teachers, especially those with handicapped children in their classes, is classroom control, the ability to manage behaviors and channel them into productive use, and to create a calm, orderly atmosphere where each person—children and teachers alike—can fulfill his or her role. Just as it is the regular classroom teacher's responsibility to improve the academic skills of mildly handicapped and low-performing children, it is also her responsibility to promote appropriate social and personal behavior and to establish an environment conducive to that behavior.

All elementary children need a classroom in which limits for their behavior are carefully delineated, expectations for desirable behavior are clear, and consequences for inappropriate behavior are communicated. All children, but particularly handicapped children, need explicit behavioral expectations provided within a warm, positive environment. Handicapped children, especially those with behavioral problems, are more likely to function appropriately in a structured, well-organized environment in which the teacher is consistent, supportive and encouraging, yet firm.

Just as children function well in an orderly classroom, so too does the teacher. While expectations for child behavior vary among teachers, most teachers need an environment in which children follow directions, are relatively quiet during instruction and independent work, are at their desks during specific activities and do not engage in physical contact with their peers (e.g., by hitting, fighting, or tripping). Teachers must take an active role in planning and implementing a behavior

Anita Archer, James Q. Affleck, and Sheila Lowenbraun

management plan within their classroom that creates this type of working environment. In designing and implementing a management program, a teacher has the right to ask children to exhibit desirable classroom behaviors. Likewise, she has the right to seek help from others (e.g, principal, parents, resource room teachers, school counselors) to establish an environment that meets her needs as a teacher and the children's needs as learners.

One of the greatest impediments to classroom management of the mildly handicapped is the belief that the problems resulting from the child's handicap prevent her from exhibiting appropriate behavior and thus from being managed in the classroom. Teachers often make comments such as:

"John can't be expected to stay in his seat. He is hyperactive."

"Sally is always talking out, getting out of her seat and refusing to do her work. I just have to remember that she is behaviorally disabled."

"Like other learning disabled children, Paul can't pay attention during instruction."

"Tom is always fighting at recess, but what can I expect with all of the problems he has."

In these examples, the teachers have dismissed the inappropriate behavior because of the children's handicaps and have established different behavioral expectations for their behavior. As a result, the teachers will be far less capable of influencing these children's behavior. Though they may need firmer behavioral limits and additional reinforcement, most mildly handicapped children can manage their own behavior and comply with classroom rules and expectations.

For example, John does stay in his seat during an interesting movie, Sally does remain quiet and in her seat when the principal is in the room, Paul does pay attention when rewarded for attending, and Tom avoids fighting when specific follow-through consequences (punishment) are outlined. (Follow-through consequences are discussed on pages 51–53.) These children can exhibit the desirable behaviors even though their performance is inconsistent. It is important to distinguish between children who *can't* control their behavior and those who *won't*. For the majority of handicapped children, the problem is *won't,* not *can't.* As a result, the regular classroom teacher, while recognizing that it may be more difficult for these children to comply, should not excuse their inappropriate classroom behavior because of their handicaps. Instead, the teacher must set expectations for classroom behaviors and assist the child in behaving appropriately.

This chapter will explore procedures that the regular classroom teacher can utilize to prevent behavioral problems and to respond to inappropriate or disruptive behavior when it occurs. The first sections focus on *whole classroom management* rather than individual behavioral programs since the well-organized, disciplined classroom provides the best atmosphere for the handicapped child. This focus on whole classroom management also recognizes that the classroom teacher can not initiate individual behavior problems, but instead must utilize procedures that benefit all children, including the mildly handicapped. Occasionally, the mildly handicapped child needs assistance beyond the procedures used for whole classroom management. In these cases, the teacher, often with the help of other staff members, will establish a special program for the child. The last section of this chapter introduces *individual behavior management programs* and how to implement them within the classroom structure.

WHOLE CLASSROOM MANAGEMENT

Preventing Behavioral Problems

Though teachers need techniques for responding to inappropriate behavior within the classroom, management should be aimed at increasing the probability that desirable behavior will occur. As a result, the teacher's primary management efforts should focus on *prevention rather than treatment* of behavioral problems. Fostering appropriate behavior involves many of the same techniques used to increase specific academic responses. Telling children what behaviors are desired, demonstrating or modeling the behaviors, and providing feedback and reinforcement for appropriate behavior are particularly important. The teacher must also communicate to the children the necessity of observing classroom rules, schedules, and specific daily routines such as leaving for recess or washing hands for lunch. An orderly classroom environment in which specific areas of the room are designated for certain activities also encourages desirable behavior.

Establishing an environment that promotes desirable classroom behavior

The first step in classroom management is establishing an environment in which desirable behavior is more likely to occur. The classroom teacher can accomplish this through the careful structuring of time and space, providing children with activities and tasks that are incompatible with disruptive or inappropriate classroom behaviors, and clearly communicating expectations for classroom behaviors.

Organizing space in the classroom. Throughout our daily lives, our physical environment communicates certain behavioral expectations to us. For example, when we enter a formal living room we behave differently than when we enter a folksy family room; we may feel apprehensive and tense in a conference room with chairs placed around a long table but relaxed and at ease in a meeting room circled with stuffed chairs or cushions. Just as these environments communicate to the adult, the classroom communicates to the child. Certainly a different message is communicated by an attractive, well-organized classroom than by a disorderly, cluttered one. The first clearly sets the stage for orderly classroom behavior and involvement in learning activities.

The teacher should not only create a general learning environment conducive to appropriate behaviors, but should delineate certain behaviors for different spatial areas of the classroom. In the floor plan shown in Figure 4.1 the teacher has, through the placement of furniture, assigned certain areas of the room for various activities. For each of the areas, she has communicated clear expectations for appropriate behavior within that space:

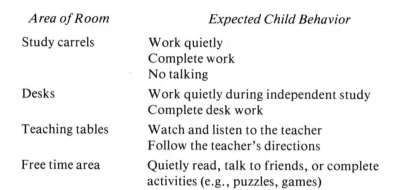

Area of Room	Expected Child Behavior
Study carrels	Work quietly Complete work No talking
Desks	Work quietly during independent study Complete desk work
Teaching tables	Watch and listen to the teacher Follow the teacher's directions
Free time area	Quietly read, talk to friends, or complete activities (e.g., puzzles, games)

FIGURE 4.1. *Spatial Organization of Classroom*

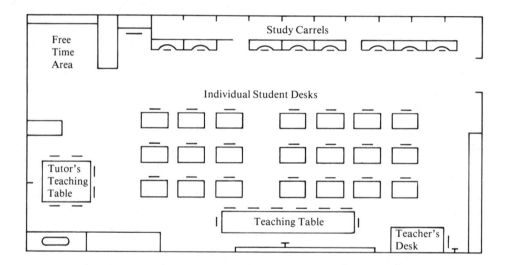

NOTE: This classroom has been arranged so that special areas are designated for specific activities accompanied by expectations for child behavior. The teacher (T) is always positioned so that she can visually monitor all areas of the classroom, which will reduce the occurrence of behavior problems (e.g., fighting between children, loud talking, wandering around the room).

Space divided in this manner reminds the child of the behavior required in each area. When the child is in the free-time area, she may engage in *quiet* conversation with peers. However, that behavior would be inappropriate at the desks during independent work sessions or at the study carrels. Likewise, talking would not be allowed during direct instruction at the teaching tables unless in response to a teacher question or direction. The teacher can also use the spatial structure to remind children of desired behaviors ("What should you do when you are at the study carrels?" "Where can we talk quietly in the room?").

When planning the spatial arrangement, the teacher should place her desk so she can face out into the classroom and maintain visual contact with students completing independent work. She should eliminate any areas in the room that can not be seen (e.g., spaces behind tall bookcases). Teachers and parents have noted that children often behave inappropriately when not in the presence of an adult.

Thus, the mere presence of the teacher is a factor in controlling child behavior. Since you are responsible for the welfare of children in your classroom, continual awareness of their activities is critical.

Organizing Time in the Classroom. Just as the physical environment promotes certain behaviors, so does the scheduling of time. Children generally perform better when a consistent routine of activities at specific times is used within the classroom. This schedule is an example for a fourth grade classroom:

8:15	Opening Activities (show & tell, lunch count, etc.)
8:30	Reading Groups
9:30	Spelling Instruction
10:00	Recess
10:15	Written Expression Exercises
10:30	Language Arts Instruction
11:00	Math Instruction
12:00	Lunch and Recess
1:00	Free Reading/Completion of Morning Assignments
1:30	Science or Social Studies
2:00	Recess
2:15	PE/Library
2:45	Music/Art
3:15	Preparation for Leaving

Within this classroom, children expect certain activities at definite times. They understand that at 10:15 they should be at their desks with paper and pencil ready for written expression. Likewise, at 8:30 the children prepare for reading instruction and either go to a teaching table or to their desks for independent work.

Consistent use of a classroom schedule not only cues children as to desired behavior, but reduces the amount of time spent by the teacher in orchestrating the class, since children are aware of what they should be doing at specific times. Just as the teacher can use the physical organization to remind children of desired behaviors, the time schedule can be used in the same manner. (''Where are you to be at this time?'' ''What supplies do you need now?'').

Since children perform far better when a routine schedule of activities is utilized, this should be established very early in the year (e.g., second day of class) and maintained even in the waning days of the school year. Though special events always occur within schools, children as well as teachers are usually more comfortable performing within a consistent structure.

Establishing Classroom Rules. Just as *telling* is a powerful procedure for providing input on how to perform academic tasks, directly telling children the behavior expected within the classroom is a simple and effective way to change behavior. To be effective, rules presented in the classroom should:

1. be very *few in number*
2. state what *behavior is desired* from the children (e.g., Complete your work. Stay at your desks. Work quietly.) rather than stating all of the behaviors you do not wish children to exhibit (e.g., Don't walk around the room. Don't hit others.)

3. be *simple and clearly stated*

4. be guidelines that you, the teacher, can *directly enforce*

You should begin by determining what needs you have in the classroom. First of all, list the types of disruptive behaviors that you do *not* want exhibited because they would interfere with the child's learning or the learning of others. Then write three to five rules that state *desired* behaviors that are incompatible with the behavior you wish to eliminate (e.g., "Keep your body to yourself" is incompatible with hitting or kicking others). Rules are best presented in terms of desirable behavior *(Do's)* rather than undesirable behavior *(Don'ts)*. When rules are presented in the form of *Don'ts*, the list would need to be endless to cover all possible inappropriate behaviors. If the list of *don'ts* did not include a specific behavior (e.g., The rules stated, "Don't hit others" but did not address kicking peers.), the teacher would have more difficulty responding to inappropriate behavior without a confrontation with the child. For example, a child with behavioral problems might respond, "But you never told us not to *kick* kids. You only said not to hit them."

In addition to being few in number and stated in positive terms, rules should be simple and clearly stated. Generally the written or verbal rule should be stated as a succinct command (e.g., work quietly). Clarity is particularly important when working with the handicapped child within the regular classroom. It is also important that the teacher can enforce the rules without reliance on reports from other children. For example, though rules for recess are also necessary, these rules should be enforced by supervisors at recess rather than the classroom teacher unless she is on "duty." When behavior is reported by another child, the information may not always be accurate and may require the teacher to spend time sorting through the stories. Though this may be necessary sometimes, it is far better for the teacher to direct enforcement at observable behaviors within the classroom.

Classroom rules should be presented on the *first* day of school. You should not wait to see what undesirable behaviors might emerge in the classroom before establishing rules. This delay in providing guidelines may lead to an increase in undesirable classroom behaviors and finally the necessity of the teacher taking firm steps to stop the behaviors. It is far more desirable to *begin* with firm, consistent expectations. If the rules are presented on the first day, the teacher will have many opportunities to provide positive feedback (e.g., verbal praise, social attention) for desirable classroom behaviors since children are generally better behaved in the first days of the school year. The rules can be presented verbally by the teacher and posted in a prominent place within the classroom. When working with handicapped children, it is often helpful to actually model the desirable behaviors for the children (e.g., "The rule is 'WORK QUIETLY.' Watch me. I am sitting at a desk doing my worksheets. I am working quietly.") as well to provide examples of noncompliance to clarify the rule (e.g., "Now I am talking to a friend. Am I following the rule? Why not?"). When the rules are stated and explained to the students, the teacher should also clearly state rewards for desired behavior and follow-through consequences for noncompliance. The children need to realize the consequences for choosing not to comply. Following the verbal presentation of the rules, the students may be asked to copy the rules in their notebooks to retain at their desk. The rules should be reviewed continually during the first weeks of school and should be reiterated by the teacher when children do not comply. Though a powerful tool, rules alone without consistent rewards for desired behavior or consistent follow-through in response to noncompliance will loose their impact. The following dialogue illustrates how rules can be presented at the beginning of the school year. (Table 4.1).

TABLE 4.1

Teacher Presentation of Classroom Rules

Mrs. Harrington on first day of school with her new group of fourth graders.

"It is my responsibility to teach as much as I can this year as well as I can. To do that I need a room that is pleasant and nice to work in where the students are quiet and working well with each other and with me. I will not tolerate any classroom behavior that does not let me teach well. You must follow these rules so we can have the kind of room I need to teach you and that you need to learn in. These are the rules that I wish you to follow this year."

The teacher refers to a chart with the rules posted in front of the room and reviews the rules with the children as well as presenting examples of desirable and undesirable behavior.

1. Follow directions.

2. Work quietly

3. Stay in your seats during instruction and seat work.

4. Keep your body to yourself

The teacher then presents the consequences for not following the rules:

"At the first offense, I will write your name on the board. This will be a reminder for you to follow the classroom rules.

"If you choose to disobey a classroom rule again, I will put a check after your name and you will be asked to work 10 minutes by yourself at the study carrels in the back of the room.

"After ten minutes you may return to your desk or to the group activity. If you again break one of the classroom rules, I will put a check after your name. If you get an additional check, you will be asked to work 10 minutes by yourself at the study carrels and 10 additional minutes at the next recess or after school.

"If your name is placed on the board and more than two checks follow your name, I will call your parents that evening to explain your classroom behavior. This is important since poor behavior in the classroom makes it difficult for you and others to learn and for me to teach."

The teacher then presents positive consequences for following the classroom rules.

"I also want to let you know when you have been working well and following the classroom rules. Here is my 'good behavior' jar. For each fifteen minutes in class in which your behavior is good with no one breaking the rules, the class will earn one penny. On Friday we will count the pennies in the 'good behavior' jar. For three pennies in the jar, the class will earn one minute for a special activity such as a party, an extra recess, a baseball game, or classroom game inside. I will really enjoy these Friday events, so I hope there will be lots of pennies in the jar. In addition to earning pennies in the jar, I will tell you about your good behavior. I will also let your parents know about your good behavior by calling them or sending them notes.

"Now let's be sure you understand the classroom rules. I am going to give you a piece of paper and I would like you to copy the rules. You should keep these rules in your desk so that we can review them in the next few days. (Children copy the rules.)

"Now I want to be sure that you understand the rules. What will happen if you choose to talk loudly in class when others are working? Right, I would write your name on the board. What would happen if later you choose to walk around the class when I was introducing new spelling words? Right, I would put a check after your name. What would you do then? Yes, you would be asked to go to one of the study carrels in the back of the room for 10 minutes. If later in the day, you hit another student, what would I do? Yes, I would again put a check after your name. What would you have to do? Yes, spend ten minutes at the study carrel and ten minutes of your recess or after school. What would I do that evening? Right, I would call your parents to describe your behavior. What will happen if the class works well for fifteen minutes? How will we use the pennies that you earn?"

The teacher continues the discussion of the rules and consequences for appropriate and inappropriate behavior. It is important that the rules are operable immediately and that the teacher follow through with the consequences. For example, if a student got up and walked to the pencil sharpener during the discussion, the teacher would *immediately* write her name on the board and reiterate the rule. Likewise, the teacher must follow through with the consequences from the first day. If the consequences are used consistently from the first day, the emphasis can be on reinforcing desirable behavior since children are generally better behaved at the beginning of the school year.

Presenting Classroom Procedures. The teacher needs to present on-going classroom procedures in the same consistent and firm manner in which she presented overall classroom rules. For example, you need to present specific classroom procedures for: entering and leaving the classroom, responding to visitors in the classroom, sharpening pencils, gaining assistance during independent work, going to the bathroom, getting drinks of water, getting school supplies, turning in completed work, gaining permission to speak in a classroom discussion, and storing personal belongings in the classroom. For example, you might establish the following procedures:

Situation	*Procedure*
Leaving the classroom	"Before recess, a special activity, lunch, or at the end of the day, I will excuse the class row by row depending on the row that is quiet and has their materials put away. When your row is excused, you may get your coat and quietly line up at the door."
Entering the classroom following lunch or recess	"When the bell rings, you should line up outside of the door. When everyone is quiet, we will go into the classroom. You should hang up your coat and take your seat quickly."
Sharpening your pencil	"There will be no sharpening of pencils when you are in an instructional group. We need that time to learn. If you need to sharpen your pencil when you are working at your desk, you may go to the pencil sharpener if no one is there."

Going to the bathroom	"I would prefer that you use the bathroom during recess or lunch. However, if you must go to the bathroom during class you may go during independent work but not during instruction."
	You need not ask me. However, if someone is out of the room, you will need to wait until she returns. See this board, it says 'out' on one side. If you go to the bathroom, turn it over so the word 'out' shows. When you return, turn the board over. If the board says 'out', you will need to wait until the person returns."
Visitors in the classroom	"When visitors come to our classroom, we continue doing our work at our desks or in group. We do not visit with the person since they usually want to see us doing our work."

Since behavior problems often occur during these daily activities, it is important that you plan classroom procedures well in advance so you can anticipate possible disruptions. Instead of presenting all of these procedures at one time, introduce them as needed. Reviewing the procedures and consistently expecting the children to comply will increase the effectiveness of the procedures, reduce potential behavior problems, and decrease time spent daily directing children in desired behaviors in these situations.

Preparing Children for Special Events. Additional behavior problems are likely to occur when the classroom routine is altered for some special event (e.g., an assembly, a school concert, a school carnival, a faculty baseball game, a field trip, a community visitor in the classroom). Handicapped children have particular difficulty managing behavior at special events (especially exciting events). For this reason, the teacher must prepare children for these activities by telling them what will occur, and what behaviors will be expected. For example, before leaving on a field trip to the zoo, the teacher should describe the sequence of events (e.g., "We will leave at 8:00 a.m. on the bus. When we arrive at the zoo, each of you will be in a small group with a teacher or parent. You will tour the zoo with the adult for an hour and half. We will then meet as a large group to see the new baby animals. After seeing the baby animals, we will return to school on the bus."), and exactly what behaviors will be expected (e.g., "When you are on the bus, you must sit quietly. When you are touring the zoo, you must stay with the adult and not leave your group."). Time spent in preparing children for such special events will reduce the possibility of inappropriate or disruptive behavior and increase the children's, as well as the teacher's, enjoyment of the activity.

Providing appropriate tasks for children

In addition to establishing a classroom structure that will facilitate appropriate behavior and explicitly stating expectations for classroom behavior, the teacher must provide appropriate tasks for children to engage in. Though behavior problems are less likely to emerge during small-group or whole-group instruction because of the proximity and direct interaction with the teacher, behavior problems often occur when children are working on independent tasks or have completed their work before the beginning of a new activity. If an independent task is beyond the child's level, or the directions are too complex, the child may become frustrated or simply not attempt the task and select other less desirable activities (e.g., talking to peers, walking around the classroom). Since task completion is incompatible with disruptive behavior, independent tasks must be carefully chosen (see Chapter 7 for a more complete description of independent tasks). It is particularly difficult to supply mildly handicapped children with appropriate independent activities because they are often working on tasks different from those of their classmates. Selection of simple workbooks, ditto sheets, programmed materials or tape recorders can increase their productivity. Resource room teachers can often be of assistance in suggesting appropriate independent work.

The teacher must also anticipate children completing work before classmates. When children do not have tasks provided for them, they are likely to engage in less acceptable and potentially disruptive behaviors. The teacher should plan specific "buffer activities," activities that the children should do when work is complete. These activities may be academic (e.g., completion of written stories for the classroom book; work on a classroom map of the United States; free reading) or nonacademic (e.g., reading magazines in the free time area; working on a large puzzle; adding to the classroom poster; completing crossword puzzles; coloring pictures). Whatever activities are chosen as buffers, they should be chosen for their ability to be used for variable amounts of time (e.g., The child may have three minutes or ten minutes between activities). The teacher should clearly specify what behaviors the children can do when work has been completed and corrected and again expect compliance with these procedures. The teacher may wish to establish an area of the room (e.g., free-time area) in which a variety of buffer activities are available for children who have completed their work. If the buffer activities are particularly appealing, the teacher will need to monitor children in the free-time area to be sure that they have carefully and accurately completed their work and corrected it if a key is available. If children abuse this privilege, their free time is removed for a day or number of days, and they are required to remain at their desks when work is complete.

Providing feedback and reinforcement for acceptable behavior

Another critical aspect of preventing behavior problems is providing positive feedback and reinforcement to children for desirable behavior. This not only reduces the probability of behavior problems occuring but creates a positive atmosphere within the classroom. Handicapped children are in particular need of firm expectations coupled with positive feedback on acceptable behavior. For them, such reinforcement is often difficult to earn, and it is essential that adults indicate frequently that they are pleased with the child's compliance.

Positive reinforcement is defined as a consequence of a behavior that increases the frequency of that behavior's occurrence. For example, if saying "Good work" to a child each time she successfully completes her math paper makes that child complete her math properly more often, the words "Good work" are a positive reinforcer. If earning pennies redeemable for minutes at a party increases a student's compliance with classroom rules, the pennies and party are positive reinforcers. However, if the pennies or praise do not increase the frequency of the behavior desired, then even though they are pleasing to the child or contribute to a nice classroom atmosphere, they are not positive reinforcers for the behaviors in question. Positive reinforcers are events or words that work to *increase* desired behavior. Many types of potential positive reinforcers are used in the average classroom. Because positive reinforcement is the backbone of any successful behavior management program, whether designed for the entire class or for a specific child, the following section will deal with various forms of positive reinforcement in the regular classroom.

Social Reinforcement. Social reinforcement or praise is the easiest and most flexible tool in the reinforcement repertoire. When a child acts appropriately the teacher praises the child verbally, referring specifically to the desired behavior. Verbal praise may be addressed either to the individual child ("John, I like the way you are working quietly." "Paul, I am pleased to see all of your work complete."), to the entire class ("Wow, you were great coming in from recess."), or to a small group ("Terrific, you are really working well together on that project." "Thank you for working so quietly at your desks. My group could really concentrate on the lesson."). To increase the impact of verbal praise, the teacher should not only pair the praise with a reference to the desired behavior, but also move closer to the child, wink or smile at him, look directly at the child when giving the verbal praise, and even touch the child. It is this nonverbal social reinforcement that communicates the sincerity of the verbal praise and personalizes the positive feedback. When working with older students who may be embarrassed by verbal praise, the teacher may wish to talk with the child alone. Social reinforcement should accompany and eventually replace the other types of reinforcement described below since it is the type most likely to occur in natural situations.

Special Activities or Privileges. Though social reinforcement is the most natural of all consequences and generally is effective in strengthening desirable classroom behaviors in students, the mildly handicapped child or the child who is having particular difficulty with behaving appropriately may need additional consequences. The following types of rewards are useful within whole class management programs or when designing individual behavior programs.

Many activities or privileges in the classroom can serve as reinforcers when they are contingent on desirable behavior. Classroom activities that many children enjoy and are easy to organize within the regular classroom include:

Erasing the board.	Correcting papers.
Feeding the class pet.	Collating papers for the class.
Taking roll.	Looking at books.
Watering the plants.	Being first in line.
Sharpening pencils for the class.	Reading to the teacher.
Handing out papers.	Collecting papers.
Running errands for the teacher.	Cleaning up the free-time area.

Taking messages to the office.

Taking the lunch count to the lunch room

Selecting books for the classroom library.

Listening to the radio, tape recorder or record player with earphones.

Phone Calls or Notes to Parents. Families of handicapped children have often been negatively conditioned to regard calls or notes from school as a sign that their child is in trouble. A positive note or call home, written or made in the child's presence, is often a tremendous reinforcer to the child as well as her family. Details of the child's progress toward or accomplishment of an academic or behavioral goal might be communicated in these ways:

Note To Parents

Dear Mr. and Mrs. Smith,

Jan and I thought you would like to know that she has reached her goal of correctly answering 35 addition facts in one minute. We are very proud of this achievement and are sending you her completed progress chart.

Sincerely,
Ms. Benson

Dear Mrs. Walker,

I have been very pleased with John's behavior this week. He has followed all of the classroom rules. I am particularly pleased with his quiet work on independent activities. I really appreciate John's help in creating a nice classroom for all of us to work in.

Sincerely,
Mr. Paynter

Follow-up Reinforcement at Home. Though this would seldom be used except for individual behavior programs, reinforcement at home for desirable behavior can often be a very powerful tool for managing child behavior. This is particularly true when rewards available in the school are not powerful enough to influence the child's behavior. For example, the teacher and parents might jointly establish a program in which the child receives special privileges (e.g., selection of dessert for the family, an extra half-hour of TV viewing, dinner out at McDonald's, a friend over on Friday) or tangible goods (e.g., a new book, a comic book, a stamp for her collection) dependent on performance within the classroom. When the parents establish any home reinforcement, consistent and clear communication must occur between the school and the home. This might be done through daily notes on performance, checklists on desired behaviors occurring during the day, or through phone calls.

Tangible Items. Tangible items can also be used as reinforcers within the classroom though they are generally less desirable than social reinforcement or special activities. Again, the items would need to be given to the child contingent on performance of desirable behavior. Items used in the classroom can be of an academic nature (e.g., pencils, colored paper, marking pens, used books from Goodwill, magazines, notebooks, lined paper) or nonacademic (e.g., pages from coloring books, crossword puzzles, edibles, stamps). However, tangible items should be used only when other effective reinforcers have not been determined through systematic use with the child. They should be paired with social reinforcement, and their use should be kept at a minimal level.

The Teacher. Yes, you are potentially one reinforcement available in the classroom. Time with the teacher, particularly on an individual basis, can be very motivating to children. This time could be spent in jointly completing an activity (e.g., assisting you in grading papers or cleaning up the room), working on an academic task with you (e.g., orally reading to you, working on a special time-telling book), or simply talking with you. Teachers have also used special events away from the school (e.g., dinner at the teacher's home, an afternoon at the park) as rewards for desirable school behaviors. Handicapped children who seek adult attention, affirmation of their personal value, and positive contact with adults are especially responsive to personal time with the teacher.

Group Reinforcement. Positive reinforcement can also be given based on the performance of the entire class. For example, the class may earn a special field trip, extra recess, a party, or other special event based on their compliance with classroom rules.

Proof of Progress Devices. All people feel more successful if there is a mechanism to remind them of how much they've accomplished. For children who find learning and compliance with classroom behavioral expectations more difficult, tangible reminders that they have succeeded in mastering new material or exhibiting a desirable behavior often encourage and inspire them to attempt acquiring a new skill or behavior. Showing tangible proof of progress includes the use of charts, checklists, or graphs which show the child how far she has come. Table 4.3 shows a sample chart on which a child's mastery of short vowel decoding is recorded.

TABLE 4.3

Individual Record of Progress on
Reading Words with Short Vowels.

GOAL: Student will read a list of words with 35 correct in a minute and no more than two errors.

Short vowel words	Date mastered	Date Reviewed
a (cat, ran)	3/2/78	3/10/78
e (bet, den)	3/15/78	3/22/78
o (mom, rob)	3/30/78	
i (sit, bib)		
u (rub, tug)		

All-purpose charts may be developed to encourage children to beat their own records for speed or accuracy in academic work. Figure 4.1 shows how a simple chart is used to record the number of arithmetic facts correctly recalled in one minute. The goal of 35 per minute correct is clearly known to the child who also can follow and actually record her progress toward that goal.

FIGURE 4.1. *Individual Chart Showing Number of Arithmetic Facts Recalled in One Minute.*

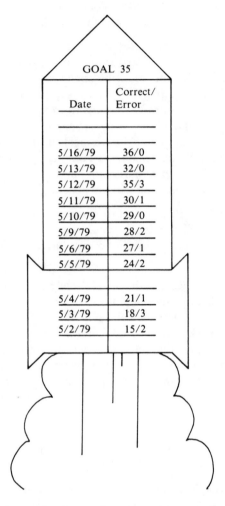

GOAL 35

Date	Correct/Error
5/16/79	36/0
5/13/79	32/0
5/12/79	35/3
5/11/79	30/1
5/10/79	29/0
5/9/79	28/2
5/6/79	27/1
5/5/79	24/2
5/4/79	21/1
5/3/79	18/3
5/2/79	15/2

Charts and graphs may also be used to record progress toward behavior goals such as working independently, arriving on time, finishing assignments, or remembering to bring homework back to school. In each case the child may be given responsibility for charting her own data, which are periodically reviewed and, if warranted, socially reinforced through praise by the teacher. When working with the mildly handicapped child or low-performing child, these charts are not publicly displayed but are kept in a notebook by the child or teacher and are private indications of progress.

Token Economies

A more complicated method of reinforcing good behavior and, possibly, punishing inappropriate behavior is the institution of a token economy. In this procedure, students earn tokens, which may be checkmarks, plastic chips, or any other intrinsically nonvaluable proof of accomplishment. These tokens are awarded contingent on the pupil's performance of various tasks or on the completion of a certain period of desired behavior—for instance, 15 minutes of reading. Tokens may be removed if the child behaves inappropriately. Tokens are redeemable for tangible reinforcers such as candy or small toys, or may be used to purchase privileges such as free time or participation in a special activity. In some cases, with the cooperation of the family, tokens earned in school may be used to purchase such privileges as T.V. watching, late bedtimes, dinners out, or movies. More sophisticated students may be given the option of redeeming small numbers of tokens for immediate gratification or saving up for purchasing a large prize such as a dinner out.

An individual token system chart for John, age 10, who is labeled mildly emotionally disturbed, might look like Table 4.4

TABLE 4.4

Contract

Name: John M.   Date: 3/14/78

Earn points for:

Coming directly to class in morning (1)	1
Sitting quietly during opening exercises (1)	1
Completing work assigned (1 each)	
reading	1
penmanship	1
math	
spelling	1
No fighting at recess (2)	
No fighting at lunch (2)	2
Total Gained	7

Lose point for:

Whining (2 each time)	
Hitting during lunch or recess	
(2 each)	2
Total Lost	2
Total Points to spend	5

Point Redemption Chart

2 points	candy
3 points	pencil
3 points	eraser
4 points	surprise box
1 point	3 minutes free time (up to 20 minutes per day)
50 points	dinner at Burger Shop

In a variation of the token system, the whole class may be involved in earning points toward a special project such as a field trip. This can put a great deal of peer pressure on class members to conform to expectations and thus not lose points for the whole class. In some cases, this peer pressure is a positive influence on the behavior of a child. In others, it may cause a child who is already a class outcast to receive even worse treatment at the hands of his peers.

When we use a token system to increase or decrease behaviors in an individual child, it is essential to keep data on the system's effectiveness. Remember, as with any other behavior control system, the tokens are positive reinforcers if, and only if, they work to change behavior. If they do not, then no matter how pleasant, stimulating, or meaningful the system is to the child, it is not effective and needs to be modified or eliminated.

Using reinforcement in the classroom

Reinforcement is a powerful tool for increasing appropriate behavior and decreasing disruptive behavior. The following guidelines will assist you in using reinforcement techniques within your classroom.

Select a Reinforcer that the Child Enjoys and Wants. Though most children respond to social reinforcement such as verbal praise, smiles, and touch, children with more severe behavior problems may require special attention. For example, the teacher might select a potential reinforcer by observing the child's preferences in the classroom. If John's favorite activity is playing four-square at recess, extra minutes at recess could be used as a reward for completing his desk work. The teacher can also draw on her knowledge of the interests of children at various age levels to assist her in selecting reinforcers. While a third grade class might work very hard to earn time to play SIMON SAYS, sixth graders might prefer time to visit with their peers. In all cases the teacher must remember that a reinforcer is defined by its *effect* on child behavior not by the actual reward. If the reinforcer does not produce improved behavior, then an alternative reward must be chosen.

Use Natural Reinforcement Wherever Possible. As already discussed, social reinforcers should be used whenever possible because of their ease of usage and their generalization to other settings. Likewise, when using other types of reinforcers, it is helpful if they are natural consequences for the desired behavior. The following are examples:

"When you finish your worksheets and correct them with the key, you may select a quiet activity in the free time area."

"Sally, if you complete all of your homework for four days, you can take home some of our color book pages to do at home instead of homework."

"If the class is quiet throughout the morning, I will read another chapter in *Charlotte's Web* after recess."

In each of these cases, there is a fairly natural relationship between desired behavior and the reward provided. Using these kinds of natural reinforcement helps avoid some of the pitfalls of using reinforcement. (See discussion of bribery in this chapter.)

Select Forms of Reinforcement that You are Comfortable with and that are Easy to Implement in Your Classroom. If you are uncomfortable using tangible items as reinforcers, select alternatives such as special activities or privileges. It is also important to select rewards that you can implement with some ease in the classroom. As previously discussed, social reinforcers are not only the most natural consequences to provide but are easy to implement within the classroom. Classroom activities such as erasing the boards and working in the free-time area might easily be used for these purposes.

Provide the Reinforcement Contingent on Desired Behavior. This guideline must be followed if rewards are to have any power in improving behavior. Certainly, an atmosphere of acceptance, respect, and warmth to *all* children is important in the classroom, but reinforcement such as praise, touch, and smiles should be paired with desired behavior. If the teacher provides the same amount of praise and social attention when children comply with classroom rules as when they choose not to comply, her praise and reinforcement will have little impact on increasing desired behaviors. For example, one teacher established the rule that children who had completed all of the assignments during the week could participate in a popcorn party on Friday while the remaining children would complete their assignments at their desk. On the first Friday, all of the children with the exception of two had completed their work. After the popcorn party began, the teacher felt sorry for the remaining children and allowed them to join the fun. On the following Friday, six children had not completed their work. The teacher responded in the same manner, inviting the remaining children to participate. It is not surprising that on the following Friday, ten children had incomplete papers since the reinforcement was given noncontingently.

When Possible, Provide the Reinforcement Immediately. To have the greatest impact on behavior, reinforcement should be given as quickly after the desired behavior has been exhibited as possible. If Molly sits in her seat throughout independent work time, the teacher should immediately praise Molly for her appropriate behavior. If she waits for ten minutes, her verbal praise might occur when Molly was talking to her friend at her desk. When reinforcement is not available immediately, the teacher can use tokens or verbal praise to bridge the time gap between the occurrence of the desired behavior and the presentation of the reinforcement. For example, the teacher has established a point system in which the children in the class are earning points for a party on Friday. Because of the delay of the reinforcement, the teacher provides verbal feedback to the children on their movement toward the goal (e.g., "Wow, the class was quiet all morning. You have already earned four minutes for the Friday party. You are really working well.") Tokens, whether checkmarks, plastic chips, or other tangible representations awarded for good behavior allow for immediate feedback to the children on desired behavior though the actual reward may be given at a later time. While older children may be able to wait three to five days for the reinforcement, younger children and children with more severe behavior problems may need to be reinforced daily in addition to the more immediate presentation of the tokens or verbal feedback.

When Rewards Other than Social Reinforcement are Used, They Should be Paired with Social Reinforcement and Gradually Faded. Fading the use of rewards can be accomplished by increasing the amount of time before a reinforcer is awarded (e.g., Mary's work is checked after a half hour rather than each fifteen minutes) or increasing the amount of behavior or work required for the reinforcer. For example, John initially earns one point for each paper completed in the classroom. He has the potential to earn ten points a day redeemable at the end of the day for a minute of recess. At first, the teacher provides the points as he completes each paper. She is careful to give verbal praise to John whenever the points are awarded. As John completes more papers, the teacher begins to check his work after every three assignments and she increases the amount of time that John must work without her praise or awarding of points. As John's work continues to improve, the amount of work needed to earn one point is increased from one assignment to two for one minute of recess. Finally, the teacher removes the point system, but continues to praise John for completion of papers. As seen in this example, time between reward and the amount of expected work is gradually increased to allow fading of the nonsocial reinforcers. At the same time, the teacher is careful to use social reinforcement for the desired behavior so that this reward can later be used to maintain the desired behavior.

Change Reinforcers if They Lose Their Effectiveness. When reinforcers are used frequently, they may loose their effectiveness. You must always remember that a reinforcer is defined by its effect on behavior rather than the reward itself. A reward that may serve to increase one behavior may not be effective for another behavior. Likewise, because reinforcers that are effective in one situation may not be effective in another, you should provide a variety of rewards within the classroom.

Plan Ahead when Using Nonsocial Reinforcers. If you select to use rewards such as special activities or tangible items, you must plan adequately before the consequences are introduced to children. This is especially true when using a token economy. You must determine the behaviors for which the tokens will be awarded, the amount of behavior needed to earn a token, the value of the tokens in relationship to the back-up reinforcers, and when the tokens will be awarded. Likewise, you must plan carefully when reinforcers are to be given at home. Meet with the parents to decide what reinforcers will be used, the behavior for which the reinforcers will be awarded, and the communication system to be used between home and school. In all cases, the reinforcement must be available *before* the system is introduced to the children so that the system is immediately operable.

Isn't this bribery?

If reinforcers are misused and applied arbitrarily they can constitute bribery. Carefully examine the following situations in which reinforcement could be termed bribery.

John and his mother enter the grocery store. As John passes the bubble gum machine, he asks, "Can I have a penny for gum?" His mother replies, "No, John." John immediately begins screaming and pulling at his mother as she moves down the aisle. Finally, in frustration, his mother kneels down and exclaims, "OK, John. If you are quiet until we leave the store, I will give you a penny." John quiets down and remains quiet until all the groceries are bagged. His mother then gives him a penny for gum. On the following Saturday the same scene is repeated . . . this time for a Milky Way candy bar.

Sally is sitting at her desk. She has in front of her a paper that she is expected to finish by the end of the hour. With thirty minutes left, none of the items have been attempted. The teacher notices that Sally is not working. She goes to her desk and says, "Sally, if you finish your paper, I will allow you to color at your desk." Sally quickly completes the paper and then colors at the desk. Later in the day, the teacher asks all of the children to take out their library books and read. Sally sits but does not take out her book.

The following sequence of events is found in both situations:

the child misbehaves,

the teacher/parent promises a reward if the child stops engaging in the undesirable behavior,

the child terminates the misbehavior,

the teacher/parent presents the reward.

When this sequence is followed, the child learns that she will be reinforced whether she behaves or misbehaves. The child also learns to manipulate the adult to get what she wants by displaying inappropriate behavior when the adult is vulnerable. This misuse of reinforcement will create a "spoiled child" who uses misbehavior to manipulate the adult into providing desired rewards.

The arrangement of reinforcers can be carefully controlled to avoid this pattern of bribery. A more appropriate arrangement is (1) to have the reinforcement established *ahead of time* so that the contingencies are not presented after inappropriate behavior is displayed, (2) use rewards that are naturally related to the desired behavior and are given more spontaneously. The following situations demonstrate a more appropriate use of rewards in which desired behavior is strengthened without reinforcement of undesirable and manipulative behaviors.

On past visits to the store, John has been noisy and disruptive. His mother, wishing to reinforce quiet behavior in the store, presents the following contingency *before* they arrive at the store. "John, I expect you to be quiet in the store. If you are quiet while I shop, you can pick out the ice cream that we will buy." As they shop, John's mother verbally praises him for being quiet. "Wow, John, it sure is fun to shop with you today. You have been so helpful and quiet. Would you like to ride in the cart?" When all of the shopping is complete, John picks out the ice cream before going to the checker.

John's mother has established the reinforcement *before* entering the store, not in response to bad behavior within the store. In this manner, John's mother is helping him to learn responsible behavior without reinforcing misbehavior. John's mother also uses the spontaneous, natural rewards of verbal praise and a ride in the cart in response to desired behavior.

> The teacher notices that Sally is sitting at her desk but is not completing her worksheet and says, "Sally, I expect you to finish those worksheets before recess. If they are not completed, you will choose to complete them during recess." Sally begins working on her papers. As the teacher moves around the room monitoring work, she stops at Sally's desk and verbally praises her for completing items on her worksheet. "Super, Sally, you have completed a whole row."

In this situation, completion of worksheets was an expected classroom behavior. Instead of bribing Sally with a reward for completion, the teacher presented a natural negative consequence for noncompletion, and immediately praised Sally when she began working on the worksheet. Sally realizes that she will only be praised when she is completing the worksheet and that failure to meet the classroom expectations will result in punishment.

Responding to Inappropriate or Disruptive Behavior

The emphasis in any classroom behavior management program should be to establish an environment that encourages appropriate behavior through the use of positive reinforcement and feedback for desirable behaviors. However, the teacher must also possess skills for responding to inappropriate behaviors when they occur in the classroom. The teacher may respond with verbal feedback on the desired behavior, with follow-through consequences (punishment), by altering the environment in which the behavior occurred, or, in certain cases, by ignoring the behavior. In all cases, the teacher will wish to use rewards when possible, and when using follow-through consequences will wish to respond with reinforcement when the desired behavior requested of the child does occur.

Verbal responses to undesirable behavior

Canter (1976) has outlined four ways the teacher can respond verbally to children to eliminate inappropriate behavior. The following examples illustrate these verbal responses to undesirable behavior (coined "verbal-limit setting" by Canter).

Behavior	Type of verbal response	Verbal response
Children talking during independent work.	Hint	"It's time to work by ourselves." "We should have a quiet class."
	"I" Messages	"I want you to begin working." "I want to see those worksheets get completed."
	Questions	"Would you please get to work?" "Class, what should you be doing?"
	Demands	"Get to work right now."

Most children will comply with the first three types of responses. The fourth type of response, demands, implies that the teacher is prepared to present a consequence for noncompliance with the demand. This type of response should be used only after the other three have failed unless the behavior is very disruptive or harmful to the child or her peers. In all cases, the teacher should state a demand only when she can actually follow through with punishment.

As with verbal praise, the impact of these responses is increased if the teacher gains eye contact with the children, utilizes gestures that imply that she means what she is saying (e.g., firm hand movement coupled with the verbal response would be appropriate, but shaking your finger at the child's face would not), uses the child's name in the verbal response ("John, sit down and begin work now"), and physical contact if the child is close to you. Again, these nonverbal behaviors increase the force of your message and show the child explicitly that you mean what you are saying. It is important that all responses to inappropriate behavior, particularly demands, are presented calmly in a firm tone of voice. In all cases, the teacher should not resort to yelling, screaming, or arguing with the child, thus communicating that you are not in control and that your behavior is less reliable.

Canter also presents excellent procedures for the teacher to follow if the child refuses to follow your command or tries in some way to dodge responsibility for his inappropriate behavior. Children will use such tactics as crying or sidetracking ("Nobody else in the classroom has to do this." "Don't get mad at me. Tom just did the same thing and you didn't tell him to stop") "You don't like me" responses ("You are always picking on me. You hate me") and belligerence ("You can't make me. I won't pick up the books. My mother won't let you push me around") are common, as is the "I'm sorry" response ("I'm sorry teacher. I promise I won't do it again, ever"). Teachers often get 'hooked' into these responses from children and back down from their original, assertive demands. Though you should respond appropriately if the child has a reasonable excuse for her behavior, you should not allow the child to maneuver you into dropping your original demand since that will weaken your future effectiveness in making requests. Instead, Canter suggests using a "broken record" strategy that has developed out of assertiveness training. When using this technique, the teacher repeats her demand, still maintaining a calm, firm manner, preceding the subsequent demands with such comments as "That's not the point. I want you to . . ." or "I understand, but I want you to . . ."). When using the broken record, the teacher repeats the demand a minimum of three times. She must be prepared to follow through with punishment if the child does not comply and in all cases *must* use the consequence that she has presented to the child. Just as backing down from a reasonable request weakens the teacher's effectiveness, failure to follow through with established consequences also erodes the teacher's ability to manage child behavior within the classroom.

Follow-through consequences (punishment).

Though all teachers would prefer not to use punishment as a part of their behavior management program, there are times when we must respond to disruptive behavior with appropriate consequences. Though punishment is usually equated with physical acts (e.g., slapping, spanking), these responses should never be used in the school, particularly in response to an inappropriate physical response (e.g., hitting, kicking, shoving) exhibited by the child. In this example, we are modeling the exact type of behavior that we do not want the child to exhibit when she is frustrated or has a problem. Punishment, however, refers to a broad class of words or actions that follow an undesirable behavior and decrease the probability of the behavior occurring again. Just as reinforcement is defined by its effect on a behavior, so too is punishment. Punishment decreases or eliminates the occurrence of a behavior and could involve such consequences as losing recess because of talking out in class, completing an assignment after school because of failure to complete during allotted time, a call to a parent following a fight in school, or time-out (brief removal from the classroom to a non-stimulating environment) when a child has ripped up a book to gain the attention of her peers.

It is very important that the teacher does not threaten children. When you make a verbal demand coupled with a follow-through consequence, you are *promising* to punish if the child does not respond appropriately. If your demand is child behavior, the children must realize that you mean what you say. Your demands and promised consequences must not be ambiguous. If you state that you will do something if a child does not comply, then you must be willing to act on your words.

Children often interpret the teacher's use of punishment as unfair. However, through her verbal presentation of demands, the teacher can clearly place the responsibility for noncompliance on the student. For example, instead of saying "If you don't stop fighting, I will take you to the office" the teacher might say, "You have a choice. Either you stop fighting right now or I will take you to the office. It is your *choice*. If you do not stop fighting you will have chosen to go to the office." When the demand is stated in this manner, the child realizes that she has actually chosen to have the consequence occur through her noncompliance. This strategy is especially useful when working with children who do not want to take any responsbility for their own behavior. They instead blame others and act as if their getting in trouble was the teacher's fault, not their own. In summary, the teacher should clearly spell out the expectations, should communicate the consequences that the child will choose if he decides not to engage in the desired behavior, and finally be fully prepared to follow through with the stated consequence if the child does not comply.

There are a number of follow-through consequences that the teacher can utilize in the regular classroom that generally will be effective, though the effectiveness of punishment just like reinforcement is dependent on the child.

Time-Out. Time-out refers to the removal of the child from a situation in which undesirable behavior is reinforced. For example, if the child talks out in class and her peers are attending to every word, removal from this environment would be an appropriate consequence. Time–out can be used for many general behaviors that could be classified as acting out or disruptive. Time–out procedures include asking the child to turn away from the small group during instruction for a short period of time, having the child leave an instructional group and work alone at her desk, or isolating the child from her peers and the teacher by placement in a secluded location in the classroom (e.g., a time-out desk in the back of the room, a chair in the corner of the room). In all cases, time-out should not be something that the child likes; it should be a time when the child is free from the attention of others. However, the child should not be totally removed from the classroom, since the teacher should be able to visually monitor the child. One way to accomplish both removal and super-vision is for teachers to cooperate on the time-out locale. For example, first and fifth grade teachers could provide a location for each other's disruptive students, who would be required to sit and work quietly at the desk in the designated classroom. In this situation, just as in your own classroom, it is important that the teacher instruct the rest of the class not to interact with the child when he is working in/or sitting in time-out.

Removal of Privileges. Another consequence that the teacher can use involves removal of privileges commonly awarded in the classroom (access to free time, recess, a school assembly, or a field trip) as a consequence for choosing not to comply with a teacher's stated expectation or classroom rule. Just as with re-inforcers, the activity must be deemed desirable by the child for it to have any effect on reducing undesirable behavior.

Staying after School. This consequence is particularly appropriate if the child has engaged in inappropriate work that has interfered with completion of classroom tasks or interfered with others completing their work.

Follow-Through Consequences at Home. We discussed earlier how parents can cooperate with the teacher to provide rewards at home dependent on their child's behavior at school. Similarly, a home privilege may be *removed* for in-appropriate behavior at school. For example, watching TV or skating on Saturday might be denied a child who has disrupted her class at school. Time-out in a child's bedroom for the amount of time not working in school might also be an appropriate consequence for poor behavior. Whatever the arrangements are, very careful planning and communication are critical in any joint school and home program.

Contacting the Child's Parents. Notes or phone calls can be made as a conse-quence for undesirable behavior. However, to avoid the pattern of all teacher contacts as being negative, the teacher should also contact the parents when desired behavior is exhibited.

Sending the Child to the Office. This is often standard procedure within the elementary school. This can be effective as a modified time-out procedure if the en-vironment is not reinforcing (e.g., attention given to the child, or there are in-teresting activities to engage in). If possible, the teacher should attempt to use follow-up consequences within the classroom. The office and contact with the prin-cipal should be used when a child exhibits exceptionally disruptive behavior in the school. To prevent the principal from acquiring a "bad person" label, the teacher should encourage other interactions between the children and the principal. For example, the principal could be invited to the class for parties, or the teacher could share information on excellent school behavior in the presence of the child and the principal.

Selecting Follow-Through Consequences. Many of the rules which apply to using reinforcement also apply to punishment. As with reinforcement, the consequences should be presented with some immediacy and should be contingent on the child's exhibition of undesirable behavior. In addition, the punishment should be applied consistently, should be of intensity proportionate to the transgression, should not be carried out when the teacher is angry, and should not be physically or psychologically harmful. It is also helpful if the follow-through consequences are pre-established in the form of a "choice" statement, so the child realizes that she is reponsible for her behavior and any subsequent punishment.

Ignoring. The response of ignoring is *only* appropriate if the behavior is being reinforced by teacher or peer attention or if the behavior is not disruptive or harmful to the child or others. However, to have any impact on decreasing the undesirable behavior, ignoring must remove *all* reinforcing attention and an appropriate behavior must be reinforced. Ignoring might be used with a child who taps her fingers on the table to gain teacher attention or pulls at the teacher's arm to gain attention.

Changing the Environment. In some situations, undesirable behavior can be reduced or eliminated by simple changes in the environment. For example, if a child is always looking out the window, you can place her desk in the other direction. If a child is quite disruptive, you can move her desk to a spot near your teaching desk. If two children are continually talking, you can separate them. If a child writes on her desk, you can place her pencils and pens in your desk and give them to her only during work sessions.

INDIVIDUAL BEHAVIOR PROGRAMS

There will be times when a child's behavior interferes with the rest of the class or with her own ability to learn, or is emotionally disturbing to the teacher and other adults. Despite your best efforts, the child's behavior does not respond to methods used with the rest of the class. When these behaviors are severe enough, effective teaching and learning can not occur. The teacher, often in cooperation with the resource room teacher, counselor, or school psychologist, can design and implement an individualized behavior program for the child. The same steps of systematic instruction outlined for teaching academic behaviors can be used in designing a behavior program.

Step 1: Initial Assessment

As with individual academic programs, your individual behavior program must be based on data collected on the child's performance. Begin by clearly defining the behavior you wish to decrease or increase so you can observe and measure it reliably. Thus, a behavior originally defined as "Susan bugs the other children" is broken down through observation into:

Susan talks to neighbors during quiet periods.
(too much talking)

Susan hits neighbors to gain attention so she can speak.
(too much hitting)

Susan throws small objects such as paper wads at other children.
(too much throwing)

A different behavior problem might initially be defined as "John is always late for class." This is broken down through obsevation into:

John walks very slowly.
(very slow rate of walking)

John stops frequently to look at wall decorations.
(too much stopping)

When observing and defining a behavior, it is also important to define the situations in which it occurred and the responses it evoked. In Susan's case, when Susan talked to her neighbors, two of them complained loudly to her and to the teacher, and one talked back to her. Here a remedy for Susan's talking might include instructing her neighbors not to respond to her efforts.

When you have defined the behavior that you wish to decrease (e.g., number of times a child hits a peer), or increase (e.g., number of assignments completed by Paul during the morning), you should collect initial assessment data (baseline data) on the frequency or duration of the target behavior for a week or until a *pattern* emerges. For example, we might count the number of papers Paul completes during math and reading period, the number of times Sue hits another child, or the total amount of time Fred spends out of his seat. As discussed in Chapter 8 on collection of data on child performance, you may measure *all* occurrences of the behavior during the school day or simply record a sample of the behavior. If the behavior occurs infrequently (e.g., swearing during the day, leaving without permission, hitting another child), you would probably count all occurrences of the behavior during the day or establish a system where the child could record her own behavior (e.g., the child marks on a tally sheet when the teacher indicates that she has talked out inappropriately). If the behavior occurs at a very high rate, thus making data recording difficult for the entire day, you may simply sample the behavior (e.g., out-of-seat behavior is only recorded during math period; talking out is recorded for a 10-minute segment each hour).

To assist the teacher or support staff in analyzing the severity of the behavior problem and in establishing an appropriate intervention program, collection of initial assessment data or baseline data is essential. These data will also be helpful in evaluating the effectiveness of the interventions initiated with the child. Baseline data collected on Susan's behavior are found in Table 4.5.

TABLE 4.5

		Talking			Throwing		Hitting	
Mon.	Read	/ / /	3	/ /	2	/	1	
	Math	/ / / /	4	/ /	2	/ /	2	
Tues.	Read	/ / /	3	/ /	2	/ /	2	
	Math	/ / /	3	/ / /	3	/ /	2	
Wed.	Read	/ / /	3	/ / /	3	⫲⫲ 5		
	Math	/ / / /	4	/ / / /	4	/ / / /	4	
Thurs.	Read	/ / /	3	/ / /	3	/ /	2	
	Math	/ /	2	/ / /	3	/ / / /	4	
Fri.	Read	/ / /	3	/ / /	3	/ /	2	
	Math	/ / /	3	/ / / /	4	/	1	

Step 2: Establishing Goals and Objectives

Using the assessment data, the teacher can establish goals and short–term objectives. These will often be included in the child's IEP, allowing all committee members, including the parents, to be involved in setting behavioral as well as academic goals and objectives for the child. As we see in Table 4.6, behavioral goals may need to be broken into a number of intermediate steps to ensure child progress.

TABLE 4.6

Child	Current functioning level	Goals and Short term Objectives
Paul	Paul completed none of the reading or math assignments during five days of baseline data.	*Goal:* Paul will complete all of the assignments given in math and reading class.
		Short–term objectives: When given an assignment in reading or math class, Paul will complete at least half of the items within the given period of time.
		Given an assignment in reading or math class, Paul will complete all items within the given time period on at least 5 of the 7 assignments.
		Given an assignment in reading or math class, Paul will complete all items within the given time period on all 7 of the daily assignments.
John	John hit another child in the classroom on an average of 10 times a day during the collection of baseline data and 15 times during each recess.	*Goal:* John will not hit peers. *Short term objectives:* (to be worked on concurrently) John will not hit any peer or have any physical contact with a peer within the classroom.
		John will not hit or have any physical contact with a peer at recess.

Step 3: Designing Your Instructional Program

Once you have determined a short-term objective to focus on, you must select interventions from those previously discussed. If you want to eliminate a behavior such as talking out, out-of-seat behavior, hitting other children, or destroying papers, you will also wish to increase a behavior that is incompatible with that inappropriate response (working quietly is incompatible with talking out, sitting in your seat is incompatible with getting out of your seat, not touching peers is incompatible with hitting others, turning in papers is incompatible with destroying papers). As a result, most behavior programs should attempt to increase a desirable behavior while decreasing an inappropriate one. In establishing the program, you should determine what reinforcers are important to the child by observing what the child selects to do during free-time and in the classroom, by asking her parents or other staff members for suggestions, or by directly consulting with the child. You will also need to determine appropriate follow-through consequences (punishment) for inappropriate or disruptive behaviors. Example programs are found at the end of this section.

An individual behavior management program should not be introduced until you carefully plan how you will use various forms of punishment. For example, if you plan to use time-out as a follow-through consequence for talking out in class, you will need to have a location isolated from classroom activities and a timer the child can use. In addition, you need to anticipate problems that might emerge during the implementation of Your Program. For example, what will you do if the child refuses to go to time-out? What will you do if the child yells and screams when left in time-out, thus disrupting any teaching activities within the classroom? After considering these questions, you may decide that you will call the principal to deal with these disruptive behaviors. In this case, make arrangements for the principal to come to the room when the child refuses to cooperate in time-out, and also have an alternate plan when the principal is unavailable. These examples are given to reinforce the necessity for carefully planning and consideration of all details before the program is actually presented to the child and implemented within the classroom.

Step 4: Implementing Your Program

Once you implement a specific behavior program, it is necessary that every adult in contact with the child hold the same expectations and use the same techniques to gain compliance. Thus, the child's regular teacher, special teachers, therapists, aides, and other school personnel who deal with the child or class need to understand clearly how the program is designed, what expectations are set for the child, and what the consequences are to the child for proper and improper behavior. If this consistency does not occur, the child will become confused or may end up manipulating one adult against another.

Many regular classroom teachers are concerned about problems with implementing an individual program with a child and not with the entire class. They often fear that the special attention given to one child will create jealousy in other children or even increase disruptive behavior in other children so that they can receive the same attention and reward. However, this is not the case. The other children in the class are well aware of behavior problems and are bothered by those who are disruptive. They want the problem child to improve behavior as much as you do and are usually glad that you are taking steps to increase the positive atmosphere of the classroom by helping the child. They also come to realize that you care about their behavior through your willingness to help the disruptive child. It is often important to explain to class members why you are introducing a program with a child and elicit their assistance in implementing the program. For example, a teacher might tell a class: "John and I are working together to reduce his talking out in class so that we will all have a better atmosphere in which to work. When John talks out, he will be asked to sit at the desk in the back of the room for fifteen minutes and complete his work. When John is at time-out, no one is to speak with him. For each fifteen minutes that John does not talk out, he will earn a point. He is collecting these points to earn certain activities in the classroom, such as time to listen to the radio. Now, this program is not going to be easy for John. I know that you would like him to do well, just as I do. We can all help by not talking to John when he should be working and encouraging him to earn a point each fifteen minutes." If the teacher is warm and positive to all children in the classroom and provides adequate positive feedback on their behavior, initiation of a special program involving reinforcement should not be a problem. If you anticipate that it might cause problems with other children, you may select to have the rewards given to the child outside of the classroom (e.g., in the resource room or at home).

Step 5: Monitoring Your Program

It is imperative that you continue data collection once you implement the program. These data are necessary for evaluation of the interventions and for program modifications. It is important that you use the program interventions for a number of days, generally not fewer than five, before you make any program modifications. In many cases, an intervention may not be immediately effective but needs to be used for some time before its effects are known. If you continually change the consequences for appropriate or inappropriate behavior, the child will become confused and your interventions may fail. Only when you are certain that your rewards are not reinforcers (there has been no increase in the desired behavior) or your follow-through consequences are not punishers (there has been no decrease in the undesirable behavior) should a program change should be made. Record and review the data daily and modify your program only when the data require it.

Many teachers are concerned about the time-consuming nature of data collection. To reduce time spent in recording data, the teacher should use very simple techniques such as maintaining a tally sheet at her desk, recording the frequency of the behavior on a piece of masking tape on her wrist, or using a simple golf counter to record the behavior. The child herself can also be trained to record the data (e.g., the child could record a plus for every assignment completed and a minus for incomplete assignments on a tally sheet at her desk; or the child could write a check on a data sheet each time the teacher verbally acknowledged earning of a check). Self-recording will make the child more aware of her behavior and more involved in the modification of that behavior. Charting and recording data on one's own behavior can also motivate change in that behavior. To increase accuracy of the data and to ensure that the child does not cheat, the teacher will occasionally need to monitor the data recording (e.g., recording data herself occasionally and comparing them to the child's data).

Summary

Individual behavior programs may be necessary when children exhibit disruptive or inappropriate behavior that interferes with their learning, the performance of other members of the class, or the effectiveness of your instruction. You should begin by defining the behavior(s) you wish to increase or decrease in precise, observable terms. You should then observe the behavior and collect data on its occurrence. This step, collecting baseline data on the behavior, should be eliminated only when the behavior threatens others in the classroom or is so disturbing to the teacher or other children that classroom activities can not proceed. These data establish the child's current functioning level, establish a basis for determining goals and objectives, and later enable the teacher to evaluate the effectiveness of the chosen interventions. After determining the exact behaviors that you wish to increase or decrease, you can write goals and objectives and design behavior programs. This latter step generally includes selection of rewards for appropriate behavior and punishment for inappropriate behavior. Thorough planning must occur before the program is introduced to the child. After implementation, the teacher must use the program consistently in all settings. The teacher must collect data on the child's behavior and should only alter the program when she is certain that the consequences are not producing the desired effects (increasing or decreasing a behavior).

Thus, successful classroom management, on both an individual and class level, helps the teacher establish a positive, orderly environment which encourages and enhances learning. Once the teacher is able to manage and direct her students' behavior in the classroom, she can then begin to apply the process of systematic instruction to academic performance.

5

Initial Assessment: Determining what to teach

Assessment consists of observing a child's behavior directly on a frequent basis. The purpose of assessment is to determine what the child can do, what the child needs to learn next, and how the child learns best. Information collected during the initial assessment phase forms the foundation for beginning instructional programming. Since assessment is an ongoing process, initial assessment refers only to the collection of new information, either at the beginning of the year, when a new skill area is introduced, or when a child enters the classroom. Although the decisions based on these initial data may change throughout the course of the year with the addition of ongoing assessment data, the initial assessment information is a crucial starting point for any new program.

Assessment, to be instructionally relevant, must focus on the direct observation of specific student behaviors. As a classroom teacher, you are the logical individual to conduct assessment because you have numerous opportunities to observe, at firsthand, children performing tasks in a natural setting. The use of an outside "tester" in a formal situation introduces two confusing variables, a stranger and a new setting, that may alter the accuracy of the data collected and even result in lower student performance. When you (the primary user of assessment information) assess a child, difficulties in communication of results between the "tester" and the teacher are eliminated. You are able to observe the entire performance, and to better relate the assessment information to instructional procedures.

Assessment is virtually meaningless if instructional programming does not follow. The information gained from these data needs to be transferred into in-

Anita Archer

structional programs for the child. In order for the assessment data to meet this criterion, only "teachable behaviors" (child behaviors you wish to change) should be assessed.

Assessment procedures should not be construed as formal diagnostic sessions. Instead, assessment should be an ongoing process of every instructional day. By directly observing child performance on a wide variety of formal and informal assessment material, you will be able to obtain the instructionally relevant information needed to begin programming. By systematically observing and recording the child's responses to carefully selected materials, you will know what the child's abilities are, what she needs to know next, and what her most effective learning strategy is.

Where to Begin

You can obtain initial information from the child's records and interviews with other professionals who have worked with the child. This initial information is then used to select more precise assessment procedures that fit the needs of the individual child.

School records

School records will usually include grade cards, anecdotal comments, and possibly skill checklists and notations concerning materials used with the child. Grade cards will usually indicate comparative status with peers and may indicate areas needing greater focus within the instructional program. Anecdotal comments often accompany grade cards or other forms found in the child's records. Though general impressions concerning the child are of some assistance, more specific notations on skills taught and methods used are of greater assistance in planning. Checklists of commercial materials used with the child are important, as the mildly handicapped child is too often reshuffled through the same materials year after year. If materials have already been used, you should find other materials for use with the child. More recently, many schools have adopted skill management systems which are criterion-referenced to indicate specific reading or math skills that the child has mastered.

A word of caution concerning the use of school records: Child performance is greatly affected by teacher expectations. You should guard against forming any negative impressions from the child's records that might interfere with working with the child. Additionally, you should remember that the information might better reflect what the child has been exposed to instead of what skills have been mastered.

Interviews with previous teachers and other professionals serving the child

The goal of all interviews with staff who are working with the child or who have worked with her is to obtain educationally relevant information that can guide selection of assessment tools and instructional activities. When attempting to detail information on "teachable behaviors," the teachers and specialists need to be asked very specific questions: "What materials were used in teaching phonics to Jane last year?"; "What decoding skills did you stress?"; "Did Jane use these skills in oral reading?"; "What basal readers did you use?" Interviews with the school psychologist, speech therapist, occupational therapist, and physical therapist add to the initial information on the child, and open communication channels that will be valuable when these services are needed for the child.

Select Diagnostic Tools for Formal and Informal Assessment

From the initial information, the specific areas to be assessed are selected for the child. Some mildly handicapped children need alternate assignments and individualized programming for all academic areas, while other children diverge from their classmates only in one or two areas. After the areas to be assessed are determined, a formal diagnostic test, an informal device you make or adapt, or systematic observation techniques are selected to obtain the assessment information. These data will be used to select objectives and instructional activities, so they need to be skill specific. The most useful information will be gained if the child's responses are not controlled (i.e., by a multiple choice format), so the work done by the child can be examined to see specific types of errors. You gain more information if error analysis is possible, and the entire process used by the child can be observed. The one-to-one situation allows you to observe *not only* the errors that are occurring but also the procedure that the child is using to complete a task. It is also helpful if the stimulus and response used for the specific task are similar to those used in the child's classroom. For example, if the usual spelling task in the classroom is to listen to a word and then write the word, this technique will provide more useful information than giving the child written words and having him examine the words to see if they are spelled correctly. Critical questions used in the selection of an assessment tool are expanded in Table 5.1.

TABLE 5.1

Guidelines in Selecting an Assessment Tool during Initial Assessment

Critical questions during selection of an assessment tool:

1. Does the tool measure specific skills?

2. Is the response made by the child independent and not a choice response?

3. Is the response demanded of the child on the subtest similar or the same type of response demanded in the classroom in that skill area?

4. Is the stimulus presented the same as the stimulus-type used for the skill area in the class?

5. Is it possible to examine the work of the child to determine specific errors that occurred?

6. Is it possible to observe the child, to examine the processes used by the child in completing a task?

7. Can the information be translated into objectives and instructional activities?

8. Does the assessment tool provide information to answer a specific question you have formulated?

9. Does the assessment tool have a wide sampling of the behavior measured?

NOTE: The above list of questions can be used in selecting assessment tools that will maximize the amount of information on "teachable behaviors."

Formal Assessment

Achievement tests

In most school districts, achievement tests are given at certain grade levels. Achievement tests have some very specific uses within the school district (such as evaluating programs or determining instructional areas needing further emphasis within a district) and may indicate general areas of a child's deficiencies, thus serving as a screening device; but they do not provide you with information that is directly useful for instructional programs for the following reasons:

1. You cannot observe the child during the exam or analyze the errors.
2. The sampling of items for each skill is very small.
3. The stimulus used and response demanded of the child is often quite different from that used in the classroom setting.

Diagnostic tests

There are numerous varieties of "diagnostic tests" that have been published commerically. These tests usually focus on a particular academic area such as reading or math. The tasks found on the diagnostic tests tend to be more skill specific, allowing the teacher to relate the information to specific programming. There is a wider sampling of specific behaviors than with achievement tests, but still a limited number of items per skill for decision-making purposes. Because the tests are usually given on a one-to-one basis with the child, diagnostic tests can include more types of responses (not just written) and more types of stimuli (not just visual). For this reason, the stimuli and responses used are often closer to those used in the classroom setting. Because the tests are given one-to-one, you can observe the entire process used by the child and analyze what types of errors are made.

Not all subtests of the various diagnostic tests are helpful in program planning and objective writing. You should carefully select subtests that are especially pertinent to the child's needs and program planning. You should begin with a specific purpose for the testing in mind or specific questions that need to be answered concerning the child, and then select an appropriate subtest. You should use subtests that adequately sample skills, have a free choice response format, and that have response and stimulus demands which are consistent with those in the classroom. The information obtained from a commerical diagnostic tool will generally best be used to indicate skill deficiencies and strengths which lead to further assessment. For example, after administering a diagnostic test in math, a teacher discovers the child's general level of functioning and some specific information as to error types. She then follows with an extensive tool she made herself that verifies or alters the original conclusions and that guides formulation of specific objectives.

There is a particular wealth of commercial diagnostic tests in the area of reading. Diagnostic reading tests will usually include some of the following subtests: vocabularly recognition, paragraph reading followed by comprehension questions, and a variety of skills (phonics, structural analysis, auditory and visual discrimination, spelling, etc.). The information gained from these tests aids in the selection of more specific tools. For example, following determinations of an approximate instructional reading level from an oral reading test and a comprehension test, a teacher might give the child an informal reading inventory (I.R.I.) for placement in a basal reader. The teacher will have an approximate grade level placement determined from the diagnostic reading test and can use this to determine a starting place on the I.R.I. From an examination of the errors on a phonics subtest the teacher may note a pattern of errors with all long vowels in the CVCe (consonant-vowel-consonant-final "e", as in *gate* and *bike*) pattern and in vowel digraphs (e.g., rain, boat). The teacher, however, wishes to further assess this area because of the thin sampling of words with these patterns found in the diagnostic reading test; she devises a skill-specific test to further assess these skill areas.

There are also a number of diagnostic tests specifically designed to assess math ability. These tests usually contain math subtests on computation, problem solving, conceptual application, and general math information. Again, you can use these tests as a starting point to direct further assessment. For example, after administering the computation subtest of a diagnostic math test, a teacher might note consistent errors in regrouping (carrying) in the four sample problems presented. The teacher might then administer a more specific, teacher-designed tool that systematically samples the child's performance on all problem types with regrouping in addition.

Placement tests

Placement tests are designed to systematically sample a child's skills in a book or educational sequence to determine where the child should be placed within the sequence. Materials usually contained in a placement test are programmed materials, basal readers, and some instructional kits. Informal reading inventories designed by publishers of basal readers present the child with a series of graduated paragraphs selected from the material in the book. The paragraphs are usually controlled as to length (100 words to 200 words). The child reads the paragraph aloud and then answers questions on the material. Accompanying each paragraph is a predetermined error criterion for word and comprehension errors. The child's performance relative to the criterion determines the child's placement.

Unfortunately, many materials do not have well-designed placement tests. Because of this, you will need to be able to formulate your own placement materials. This is particularly significant for the handicapped child for whom no assumptions concerning grade level placement or performance can arbitrarily be made.

Informal Assessment

Informal assessment tools include teacher-made skill tests, teacher-made placement tests for commercial materials, and structured observations in the classroom. Informal assessment is often used as a follow-up of commercial diagnostic tests. Because you create or adapt these tools, they often more closely match your assessment needs and the materials available for instructional purposes. You design the tools so that they have a wide sampling of the desired skill, allow one-to-one observation, employ stimuli and responses that are used in the classroom, and allow for error analysis. The information obtained from informal assessment thus helps determine even more precisely which forms of instruction will benefit the handicapped child.

Skill-specific tests

Skill-specific tests may be designed to measure a very small area of school behavior. For example, you may wish to look carefully at activities such as writing numbers from one to ten, solving multiplication facts to five, or using punctuation in sentences. You then structure a situation that forces the child to attempt to perform the desired behavior. For example, you might give the child a series of thirty-five sentences demanding a period, question mark, or exclamation mark. These very specific tests lead directly to establishing an objective and indicate the type of instruction necessary. The type of test might be administered throughout the year prior to initiation of instruction in a certain area. Often this type of specific skill test is used as a pre- and post-measure of skill attainment (see Tables 5.2 and 5.3).

TABLE 5.2

Skill-specific Test

Decoding of words with short vowel *i*

	Directions to Teacher: Have the child read the words and sentences orally. Record the exact pronunciations of the child.

*CVC words	①	bin	dip	fin	hip	jib	kit	mix	pig	rib
CCVC words	②	brim	flip	skid	slit	thin	twig	whip	whiz	
CVCC words	③	dish	fist	gift	hint	lick	risk	wick	wind	
Two-syllable divided words	④	frig id	in still	lim it	mim ic	mis fit				

Words in sentences	⑤	Dick and Jim will go on the ship. The ship is made of tin.
	⑥	Jim and Dick will get fish on the ship.

*CVC: consonant-vowel-consonant

NOTE: Teacher-made skill-specific tests look at only one skill element. They are often used before initiating instruction and then as a follow-up measure after the skill has been taught.

Sequence-based tests

Often you will want to examine a series of related skills that are graduated in difficulty. For example, you may wish to measure addition skills of many problem types, or to examine all of the phonetic decoding skills. It is best if you begin formulating a sequence–based test with a skill sequence—a graduated listing of the skills from the least complex to the most complex. You can generate these sequences or use a predetermined one. Skill sequences can be found in college texts on the various academic areas, in teacher resource materials, in scope and sequences for commercially published materials, or in the newer skill management systems and criterion-referenced tests. You may wish to supplement and add steps to any of the predetermined sequences. Often such sequences are written with the normally progressing child in mind and will not include a fine breakdown of skill steps needed by the handicapped child. One example of such a skill sequence in the area of writing is discussed in Chapter 6.

TABLE 5.3

Skill-specific Test

Dividing by one-digit divisor into two-digit dividend with and without remainder

Directions: Solve each problem.

ROW 1: $4\overline{)24}$ $5\overline{)35}$ $7\overline{)49}$ $8\overline{)40}$

ROW 2: $5\overline{)36}$ $8\overline{)50}$ $5\overline{)32}$ $9\overline{)83}$

ROW 3: $6\overline{)72}$ $5\overline{)65}$ $7\overline{)91}$ $3\overline{)42}$

ROW 4: $8\overline{)97}$ $3\overline{)44}$ $6\overline{)74}$ $3\overline{)53}$

NOTE: This teacher-made test evaluates one skill area, division by a one-digit divisor into a two-digit dividend. However, the items selected are arranged so that each row examines a different problem type: Row 1, one-digit into two-digit, one subtraction, no remainder; Row 2, one-digit into two-digit, one subtraction, remainder; Row 3, one-digit into two-digit, two subtractions, no remainder; Row 4, one-digit into two-digits, two subtractions, remainder. This organization allows you to determine specific error patterns.

After you formulate a sequence, select items that will measure each defined skill. Arranging items in the order of the established sequence will help determine exactly where the child's skills begin to weaken and where instruction should begin. The sequences established for diagnostic purposes will also be used later in guiding instruction for the child. Examples of sequence–based tests are given in Tables 5.4, 5.5, and 5.6. In each of these examples, note the sequential steps examined, the type of items selected to measure performance, and the ordering of the items.

Teacher-made placement tests

Placement tests determine where a child should begin instruction by sampling skills and tasks demanded throughout a material graduated in difficulty. These tests use the technique of presenting samples of items found in the material in the same order as the material. If the material has been carefully sequenced from least complex to most complex, the sampling of tasks within the material should indicate where the child is having difficulty and subsequently indicate where the child should begin work within the material.

Because available commerically designed placement tests may not be suitable for a particular child's needs, you as a regular classroom teacher may have to modify or create your own placement test. To create a placement test you simply go through a material graduated in difficulty, selecting a sample of tasks for each different step presented in the material. To increase the usefulness of these tests, you should present items in the same manner as the material. For example, if you wish to design a placement test for a spelling book, you might select every fifth word from each list found in the three spelling levels at which the child is performing. You would administer the words until the child experienced substantial failure. You would then examine the words spelled, determine where the child began missing the words, and determine a placement point in the material.

TABLE 5.4

Sequence-based Test

A teacher-made test for addition operations

Sequential Steps:		Problems:		
Step 1: 2 digit + 1 digit, no regrouping	42 +5	38 +1	72 +6	51 +6
Step 2: 2 digit + 2 digit, no regrouping	33 +25	48 +21	36 +22	87 +12
Step 3: 3 digit + 1 digit, no regrouping	342 +5	463 +5	823 +6	792 +7
Step 4: 3 digit + 2 digit, no regrouping	825 +23	925 +32	782 +16	571 +28
Step 5: 3 digit + 3 digit, no regrouping	802 +195	362 +403	723 +156	892 +105
Step 6: 3 one digit, no regrouping	3 +4 2	6 +1 2	2 +1 4	
Step 7: 4 one digit, no regrouping	2 +0 1 3	4 +2 1 1	3 +2 1 3	
Step 8: 2 digit + 1 digit, regrouping	43 +7	69 +7	38 +5	27 +9
Step 9: 2 digit + 2 digit, regrouping to 10's	38 +27	43 +29	59 +25	26 +35
Step 10: 2 digit + 2 digit, regrouping to 100's	42 +81	64 +83	92 +93	47 +82
Step 11: 2 digit + 2 digit, regrouping	38 +92	67 +85	39 +47	83 +65

NOTE: This is the first page in a sequence-based test developed for assessment of addition computations. The items were selected to match each step on a sequence developed for the instruction of addition operations.

The same technique could be used for placement in a math book. You select the math texts for grades one, two, and three. By systematically reviewing the texts, you can extract items which sample the skills presented in the material. Many commercial materials are *multi-strand*; that is, the material focuses on more than one skill area for a specific academic subject. For example, a math book might include computations, problem solving, money, time, and geometry. A handicapped child's skills may vary widely across these different strands. For this reason a single point placement into material is often not appropriate. Instead, placement points in a time–telling sequence, a subtraction sequence, a money and a problem–solving sequence might be necessary in a math book.

TABLE 5.5

Assessment for Lowercase Letters (small letters)

1. Ask your student to write the following letters when given the verbal name. You may have the child write the letters next to a manuscript letter; however, this this does cue letter formation. (These are organized into groups based on starting point and initial stroke.)

   a. Write a small *e, f, l, k, h, b*

   b. Write a small *a, g, q, c, d, o*

   c. Write a small *i, j, p, t, u, w*

   d. Write a small *m, n, v, y, z, x*

   e. Write a small *r, s*

2. Select those letters the child cannot write when verbally given the name of the letter and see if the child can copy the letter when given a written model.

3. Select those letters the child cannot copy from a written model and see if he can trace over the model accurately.

4. Fill in a record sheet. For each letter check the appropriate box.
   TR = trace   *CP* = copy   *WR* = write   *FL* = fluency

	WR	CP	TR		WR	CP	TR
e				j			
f				p			
l				t			
k				u			
h				w			
b				m			
a				n			
g				v			
d				y			
q				z			
c				x			
o				r			
i				s			

NOTE: This is another example of a sequence-based assessment tool. The teacher has grouped the lowercase letters by similarity of formation. She assesses the writing of these letters with no model present; the copying of the letters using a model; and finally the tracing of the letters.

TABLE 5.6

Sequence-based Test

A teacher-made test for syllabic analysis

Entry Skills:

1. *Decodes one syllable words* (phonetically regular words).
   Administer phonics test.

2. *Counts the number of syllables in a word.*
   Directions: "Listen as I say these words. How many syllables do you hear in the
     word?"
   bedroom   afternoon   circus   elephant   grandmother   situation
   camel   garden   football   chair   group   hassle   play   typewriter

3. *Defines a syllable as a letter or group of letters with one vowel sound.*
   Directions: "Circle the groups of letters that can be a syllable."
   in   sh   rea   to   str   in   fue   ch   spr   fi   foin   gro

~~~~~~

Screening Test

Syllabic analysis: "Read these words." (You may have child mark in division of syllables
     after he has orally read the words.)

Pattern:	*Example Words:*						
*VC/CV	goddess	hammock	offend	robbing	traffic	button	snobbish
	infect	hotbed	consult	cosmic	Baptist	absent	dispel
	anthem	crabgrass	dustmop	endman	minstrel	obstruct	oppress
V/CV	pilot	station	clover	pupil	secret	decide	donate
VC/V	melon	comic	cabin	pedal	second	robin	seven
/CLE	fizzle	needle	nestle	kindle	stumble	tackle	crumble

*V = vowel   C = consonant

NOTE: This sequence-based assessment tool was designed to measure a child's ability to use syllabic analysis skills. The test begins by assessing needed entry level skills. The test then samples the child's ability to decode words with various patterns: VC/CV pattern with identical consonants: VC/CV pattern with non-identical consonants; VC/CV pattern with blends and digraphs; V/VC pattern; VC/V pattern and the /CLE pattern. The patterns are arranged in the order that you would introduce the patterns for syllabic analysis.

Basal readers also include many skill strands; for example, vocabulary recognition, comprehension, phonics, structural analysis, contextual analysis, and study skills. At certain points in the basal, the child is expected to have acquired certain levels of achievement across all strands. This simultaneous achievement across strands seldom occurs even in normal learners; the handicapped child most often has very different achievement levels in these strands. For this reason, the basal reader is often used for only a limited number of skill strands, with other strands taught separately according to the individual child's needs. When this is the case, the placement test should reflect the strands the teacher has chosen to use in the basal reader. The strands chosen will usually be word recognition and comprehension because of their dependence on story content, with word–attack skills taught separately from the progression of the basal reader.

To augment the usefulness of the placement test, you can use the procedures discussed under sequence-based tests. You will not only have a well organized assessment tool, but a skill sequence that can be used in program planning and monitoring progress.

Use of classroom activities

There are some very simple initial assessment techniques which are often overlooked, but which are important because of their ease of use within the regular classroom. You will often have a wealth of commercial instructional materials available, including workbooks, basal readers, accompanying workbooks, and other texts. All of these materials include review exercises for certain skill areas which the teacher can draw on in the initial assessment procedures. For example, you might select the review pages on computational skills out of the second and third grade math books. After the child has completed the review pages, you can examine the work carefully for recurring error types and locate where the child should begin instruction or further assessment. This use of review exercises for assessment purposes can be followed by a test you have made to examine more specific skills or to gain a wider sampling of the behavior. You can follow up the review pages with other pages from the material that focus on a problem type missed by the child. For example, a second grade teacher wishing to assess initial phonics skills might begin by giving the child review sheets from the end of the phonics workbooks used in class. If the child missed certain consonant items, the teacher could give the child one sheet on each of the letters missed to determine if any particular phoneme-grapheme relationship would require individual instructional time.

After completing formal or informal assessment procedures, you may need very specific information on one skill. Again, draw from exercises available in commercial materials. For example, after giving an informal reading inventory, a teacher noted that the child consistently missed comprehension questions demanding more than a literal response. The teacher asked the student to answer the written questions that followed a paragraph in a basal reader workbook. The paragraph focused on a main idea and involved an extension of ideas. The child's ability to answer these questions was then assessed by the teacher.

Systematic observation

You do not always have to use a structured paper-and-pencil task for initial assessment purposes; often that type of testing is not appropriate for specific tasks. You can simply ask the child to perform a task and examine the child's performance carefully. For example, this technique would be appropriate for assessing self-help skills or gross motor skills. You would direct the child to: "Put on this coat," "Color in this picture," "Stack these blocks," or "Write this letter." You might wish to record the results of the child's performance in a simple checklist. You may wish to add anecdotal comments to explain the exact performance of the child. Any observation technique is improved if you have a specific reason or formulated question in mind to guide the observation, and if you collect data over time (see Tables 5.7 and 5.8).

TABLE 5.7

Observation of Cursive Writing
Checklist

Name_____

Directions: Ask the child to copy a paragraph printed in manuscript using cursive writing. Observe the child, noting the following behaviors.

yes no   1. Is the pencil held correctly (grip)?

yes no   2. Is the paper positioned correctly?

yes no   3. Are lower case letters formed correctly?

yes no   4. Are upper case letters formed correctly?

yes no   5. Are cursive letters correctly connected?

yes no   6. Do the letters rest on the baseline?

yes no   7. Do the letters have a correct and consistent midline?

yes no   8. Do the letters have a correct and consistent top line?

yes no   9. Is the slant of the letters appropriate and consistent?

yes no   10. Is the spacing between letters appropriate and consistent?

yes no   11. Is the spacing between words appropriate and consistent?

yes no   12. Is the handwriting neat?

yes no   13. Is the handwriting easy to read?

yes no   14. Does the child write fluently?

Comments: _____

_____

NOTE: Systematic observation can be used for many academic and nonacademic behaviors. Here the teacher carefully observes the child's cursive writing and notes specific deficiencies that need direct instruction. The teacher might later use this checklist to gauge the child's growth in handwriting.

TABLE 5.8

Analysis of Expressive Writing

Child_____ Type of writing analyzed_____

Rating scale: 1   2   3
                  poor   adequate   excellent

CONTENT

1 2 3   A. Does the writing clearly communicate an idea or ideas to the reader?

1 2 3   B. Is the content adequately developed?

1 2 3   C. Is the content interesting to the potential reader?

VOCABULARY

1 2 3   A. Does the writer select appropriate words to communicate his/her ideas?

1 2 3   B. Does the writer use precise/vivid vocabulary?

Rating scale: 1   2   3
                                poor   adequate   excellent

 1 2 3   C. Does the writer effectively use verbs, nouns, adjectives and adverbs?

 1 3 3   D. Does the vocabulary meet acceptable standards for written English (e.g., "isn't" vs. "ain't")?

SENTENCES
 1 2 3   A. Are the sentences complete (subject and predicate)?

 1 2 3   B. Are run-on sentences avoided?

 1 2 3   C. Are exceptionally complex sentences avoided?

 1 2 3   D. Are the sentences grammatically correct (e.g., word order, subject-verb agreement)?

PARAGRAPHS
 1 2 3   A. Do the sentences in the paragraph relate to one topic?

 1 2 3   B. Are the sentences organized to reflect the relationships between ideas within the paragraph?

 1 2 3   C. Does the paragraph include a topical, introductory or transition sentence?

MECHANICS
 1 2 3   A. Are the paragraphs indented?

 1 2 3   B. Are correct margins used?

 1 2 3   C. Are capitals used at the beginning of sentences?

 1 2 3   D. Are additional capitals used as necessary in the written sample?

 1 2 3   E. Is correct end of sentence punctuation used?

 1 2 3   F. Is additional punctuation used as necessary in the written sample?

HANDWRITING
 1 2 3   A. Is the handwriting legible?

 1 2 3   B. Is the handwriting neat?

SPELLING
 1 2 3   A. Does the writer correctly spell high frequency, irregular words?

 1 2 3   B. Does the writer correctly spell phonetic words?

NOTES: Using these guidelines, the teacher can carefully examine a child's written work and pinpoint instructional needs. For example, it might be determined that the child needs instruction on writing complete sentences, using correct punctuation or proofing for spelling errors. Evaluation of more than one sample would increase the accuracy of these conclusions.

Observation of social behaviors—cooperative play, compliance, following directions—can best be assessed by specifying the desired behavior and counting occurrences of that behavior during various periods of the day. This information is used, as are all assessment data, to formulate instructional programs for children. (see Table 5.9)

TABLE 5.9

Systematic Observation Record: Classroom Behavior Problems

Child: *Mary*

Time/Comments	Out of seat	In seat	Working on assigned paper	Not working	Interacting with peer	Interacting with teacher	Interacting with adult volunteer	Verbalizing
9:00 Mary is out of seat asking aide for help in math assignment.	X			X			X	X
9:02 Mary still talking with aide about math assignment. Teacher tells Mary to go to seat.	X			X			X	X
9:04 Mary is moving toward her desk. Is talking with Mark. Teacher tells Mary to go to seat.	X			X	X			X
9:06 Mary is near her desk talking to Susan. Teacher says "SIT DOWN."	X			X	X			X
9:08 Working on math paper.		X	X					
9:10 Looking around room.		X		X				
9:12 Talking with aide, asking aide to correct math problem.	X			X			X	X
9:14 Talking with aide; wants a different pencil. Teacher says "Sit down."	X			X			X	X
9:16 Mary asks teacher "How many problems should I do? Have I done enough?" Teacher replies, "Do ten. Sit down."	X			X		X		X
9:18 Working on math paper.		X	X					

NOTE: Systematic observation is particularly useful in examining classroom behavior problems. This observation data sheet was designed to analyze Mary's classroom behavior. The teacher was particularly concerned about out-of-seat behavior and the lack of work completed in the classroom periods. Every two minutes the teacher would look up and make notations concerning Mary's behavior. The teacher continued this observation technique for five days until she had discovered a pattern in Mary's behavior.

Error Analysis

After collecting the initial assessment data, you need to examine the data closely to determine the errors the child is making. Skills that the child cannot perform at all are noted. Consistent incorrect responses are very important, because they give specific clues for extra instruction. For example, in examining a child's response to add facts with sums zero to eighteen, you may find that the child's errors occur only when the sum is greater than ten. Specific items need to be examined in order to locate a pattern of errors that occurs in the performance of a specific skill. For example, following a test on regrouping (borrowing) in subtraction, a teacher examined the problems closely and discovered that the child borrowed on each problem, whether borrowing was needed or not. Another child perhaps missed the same number of items on the subtraction with a regrouping subtest, but the errors occurred when the child mistakenly began on the left side of the problem and moved to the right. The two children might have missed the same items because of faulty knowledge of subtraction facts. This teacher must now examine the items carefully to locate the type of error in order to correct the difficulty (see Tables 5.10 and 5.11).

TABLE 5.10

Error Analysis of Jimmy's Performance on Teacher-Made Addition Survey

Name: _Jimmy_

$\begin{array}{r}24\\+\ 3\\\hline 27\end{array}$	$\begin{array}{r}15\\+31\\\hline 46\end{array}$	$\begin{array}{r}430\\+123\\\hline 553\end{array}$	$\begin{array}{r}3671\\+1220\\\hline 4891\end{array}$	$\begin{array}{r}2\\3\\+4\\\hline 9\end{array}$
$\begin{array}{r}42\ \checkmark\\+\ 8\\\hline 410\end{array}$	$\begin{array}{r}92\ \checkmark\\+\ 8\\\hline 910\end{array}$	$\begin{array}{r}46\ \checkmark\\+25\\\hline 611\end{array}$	$\begin{array}{r}38\ \checkmark\\+72\\\hline 1010\end{array}$	$\begin{array}{r}207\ \checkmark\\+\ 5\\\hline 214\end{array}$
$\begin{array}{r}392\ \checkmark\\+\ 9\\\hline 3911\end{array}$	$\begin{array}{r}467\ \checkmark\\+28\\\hline 485\end{array}$	$\begin{array}{r}295\ \checkmark\\+\ 38\\\hline 21212\end{array}$	$\begin{array}{r}5\\+8\\6\\\hline 19\end{array}$	$\begin{array}{r}3\\5\\+4\\6\\\hline 18\end{array}$

Specific errors: Jimmy began making errors on problems involving regrouping in addition. He treated each problem as a set of column additions, adding each column separately. Errors were made on two facts (7 + 5 =, 5 + 8 =).

Teacher's observations: Though the addition problems with no regrouping appear correct from examination of the completed survey, on direct observation the teacher noted that Jimmy proceeded from left to right on each problem. This pattern continued through the more difficult problems. Though Jimmy was fairly accurate on addition facts, he was very slow in obtaining the correct answer. He used counting procedures to determine all answers on facts. It appears that Jimmy has been exposed to the idea of regrouping, though he has not mastered the concept. After finishing each problem demanding regrouping, Jimmy went back and added *ones* above the columns.

Conclusions: Further assessment is needed on addition facts. A technique controlling for time should be used. Instruction should attempt to increase the rate on addition facts and on two-digit–plus–one-digit problems with no regrouping. Correct movement from right to left should be stressed.

TABLE 5.11

Error Analysis of Tanya's Performance on Sight Vocabulary List

Initial Assessment: Present words in tachistoscope. Give the child a half-second initial exposure. Write down the child's response. If error was made or the child made no response, give the child a longer exposure to the word and record her next response.

flash	word	unlimited		flash	word	unlimited
ă	able	+		be	between	DK
out	about	+		+	big	
a	above	abov		+	black	
ac	across	+		DK	board	DK
af	after	+		+	book	
ă	again	a gāin		brat	both	DK
				+	boy	
+	all			brat	brought	—
* DK	almost	al mŏst		+	but	
ă	alone	ă lōne		+	by	
DK	already	DK		all	called	call
way	always	+		can	came	come
+	am			+	can	
+	an			can	car	—
+	and			chip	change	DK
an	another	DK		+	children	
an	any	+		ch	church	+
+	are			+	city	
+	around			clop	close	DK
and	art	+		came	come	+
+	as			come	company	DK
+	ask			DK	country	DK
+	at			can	could	+
+	away			+	cut	
+	back			+	day	
+	be			+	days	
be	because	DK		+	did	
b	been	bēen		did	didn't	did not
be	before	DK		DK	different	DK
DK	behind	be/DK		+	do	
be	believe	be/DK		da	does	does
+	best			DK	done	done
bet	better	+		da	don't	do not
da	door	+		fĭ	find	+
+	down			fast	first	DK
DK	each	+		+	five	
DK	early	—		+	for	
+	end			out	found	DK
DK	enough	—		+	four	
e	even	—		form	from	+
DK	ever	—		DK	front	fr/DK

TABLE 5.11 (cont.)

Error Analysis of Tanya's Performance on Sight Vocabulary List

DK	every	—		*fell*	full	+		
eye	eyes	+		*give*	gave	+		
+	face			+	get			
fair	far	*fair*		+	girl			
fill	feel	+		+	give			
+	feet			+	go			

    *+   Correct   —   No response   DK   Indicated that she did not know the word.

Specific errors: On the flash presentation of words, which is a good measure of words that Tanya can instantly recognize, she missed these specific words: able, about, above, across, after, again, almost, alone, already, always, another, any, art, because, been, before, behind, believe, better, between, board, both, brought, called, came, car, change, church, close, come, company, country, could, didn't, different, does, done, don't, door, each, early, enough, even, ever, every, eyes, far, feel, find, first, found, from, front, full, gave.

Teacher observations: As hypothesized from her slow, labored oral reading, Tanya has a very limited sight vocabulary. On this test, she missed the majority of words presented with limited exposure to the word but was able to decode more words when given an unlimited exposure to the word. If she did not know the word instantly, she either responded with an incorrect response or the comments, "I don't know it." "I haven't learned it yet." Tanya often responded with the first part of the word when presented a word using a flash procedure. For example, for the word *better* she responded *bet*. It appeared that even on the flash presentations, she attempted to phonetically decode the words. On the words that she pronounced correctly, she would often repeat the words over and over before pronouncing for the teacher, finally blending the sounds together. On many of the words that Tanya mispronounced on the flash presentation, she responded with a word that had a similar appearance. For example, she substituted *fair* for *far, all* for *called,* and *fell* for *full.*

Conclusions: Begin instruction on the words missed during the flash presentation on the test. Set a criterion of mastery on each word that demands recognition within a half-second to guarantee that she is recognizing the words by sight. In teaching the words, use procedures that stress visual memory and quick recognition of the words. Present the words in both practice sentences and phrases.

Some Final Words on Initial Assessment

Having accepted the necessity of initial assessment for the handicapped child, you will need to establish some practical methods of carrying out assessment within the structure of the regular classroom. Many of the procedures previously discussed can be carried out during independent work sessions within the classroom. For example, selected worksheets used for assessment purposes could be assigned during a work session. Tasks requiring an oral response could be adapted to a tape recorder. For example, the child could read a word list onto tape that could be evaluated for correct and incorrect reponses. The tape recorder could also be used to give oral stimuli to the child. The child could take a preliminary spelling test using a tape recorded list of words.

As previously discussed, the value of assessment is increased if you can observe the process the child uses in responding. For example, you might note that a child is not carrying in addition. But on closer observation, you might realize that the child is proceeding from left to right instead of from right to left. Oral reading and decoding skills are best evaluated in structured tasks where you are observing the oral reading of the child. These sessions demanding teacher-student interaction can be carried out in part during class time. You can work independently with the child during a seat-work session or as a part of a small-group instruction. You should not, however, remove the child from art, recess, music, or physical education activities for assessment purposes. The child may feel punished and not perform at his or her maximum. It is often desirable to have the child come to a special assessment session before or after school, when you can work with the child without the pressure of classroom activities. You can often establish a special rapport with the child during the one-to-one session.

The performance of a child on "one-day" assessment activities can be affected by many factors that might significantly alter the child's performance, such as illness, desire to engage in other activities, or fear of failure. In all cases, the original decisions made from the initial assessment data should be continually updated and altered in relation to the daily assessment data. When assessment is viewed as an on-going process, you are assured of always knowing what the child can do and what the child needs to learn to do next.

Often a teacher's first reaction to a discussion on initial assessment is that it is time-consuming and could not be accomplished within the regular classroom. Though initial assessment is an important basis for teaching all children in the classroom, it is imperative for the mildly handicapped child. No assumptions can be made concerning grade level progression or "usual skills" possessed by such a child. For the handicapped child, time in school must be used to the fullest extent possible. Work that is too easy is assigned to the handicapped child as often as work that is too difficult. Because the information collected during initial assessment will guide you in formulating a blueprint of instruction for the child, it is important that the information be accurate and complete.

Summary

In summary, initial assessment answers the questions "What can the child do?" and "What does the child need to learn to do next?" Because you as a teacher have daily contact with children in natural settings, you are the most appropriate person to collect this information on an ongoing basis. Commercial diagnostic tests, systematic observation, and teacher-made instruments are just a few of the techniques available for your use.

Since the regular classroom teacher will be utilizing commercially prepared materials with most low-performing children, the most critical type of assessment involves placement within an instructional sequence and measurement of the child's current functioning level on the skills presented in the material. You can measure the child's performance in relationship to a specific text or material by sampling items from the material and presenting them to the child; extracting the skill sequence from the material, designing measurement items to match the sequential steps, and administering them to the child or groups of children; or presenting the child with review exercises from the material to determine the child's current functioning level. Whether teacher-made or commercially-prepared tests are used, the items should measure "teachable behaviors" and the information collected should lead directly to program planning and instruction. To increase the accuracy of the assessment, the items should resemble classroom activities, the child should make a free response (not a forced-choice response such as multiple choice items), the number of items should be adequate for decision making, and the child's responses should be preserved so that an error analysis can be conducted.

6

Determining Goals and Objectives

Once you have assessed the exact skill levels of the mildly handicapped child in your class, you can translate this information into meaningful school activities that meet the needs of each child and fit into the overall goals of the classroom. To accomplish this task, you must set clear annual goals (where you would like the child to be at the end of the year), establish sequential steps leading to each goal, and translate these steps into short-term objectives. Though teachers always have goals and objectives in mind when presenting instruction or practice activities, it is helpful to formalize these steps in writing when working with the low-performing or mildly handicapped child. This is particularly important when the instruction is different from that being introduced to other students in the class. When you formally establish annual goals, you will have a "road map" that directs the child's instruction, allows evaluation of his progress, and encourages open communication concerning the child's instructional program among other professionals and the child's parents.

For these low-performing and mildly handicapped children, you will also need to specify sequential instructional steps that lead to mastery of the annual goals. When you write out the sequence, you can modify it to meet the needs of the child and use it in daily program planning and monitoring. Although this task is time consuming initially, the precision it adds to instruction benefits both the teacher and the handicapped child.

The work upon which portions of Chapters 6 and 7 are based was performed pursuant to Contract 300-75-0043 (Bureau of Education for the Handicapped) for the Northwest Learning Resources System and the Montana State Department of Education and was originally published in the following paper:

Archer, A. *Instructional materials for the mildly handicapped: Selection, utilization, and modification.* Eugene, Oregon: Northwest Learning Resources System, 1977.

SETTING ANNUAL GOALS

Annual goals state the skill areas in which the child should be proficient at the end of the school year. Though yearly goals are primarily designed to provide an "instructional road map" for teachers to follow, they are also important in evaluating the success of the instructional program, in guiding you as you make instructional modifications when the students are not progressing satisfactorily, and in communicating with the child, parents, and other professionals.

The following goals, in Table 6.1, were established for Molly, a sixth-grade learning-disabled student who attends a regular sixth-grade class in addition to a special education resource room.

TABLE 6.1

Annual Goals Established for Molly

Math	Will solve addition and subtraction facts.
	Will solve addition problems involving 3 digits plus 3 digits with regrouping.
	Will solve subtraction problems involving 3 digits minus 3 digits with regrouping.
	Will tell time to the minute.
	Will count money up to values of $10.00.
	Will solve multiplication facts.
	Will label fractional parts of sets and wholes.
Reading	Will decode phonetically regular one-syllable words.
	Will decode words with common inflectional endings.
	Will recognize instantly the basic vocabulary presented in Ginn 720, level 8.
	Will answer literal comprehension questions on a passage written at the 2.5 reading level.
	Will orally read 90 words per minute in the Ginn 720 level 8.
Handwriting	Will form letters and words using cursive.
Written Expression	Will spell irregular words on Dolch list through level 3.
	Will spell words presented in *Growth in Spelling, Green Book* (Laidlaw Brothers, 1975).
	Will write series of related sentences in paragraph form.
School behaviors	Will increase amount of time of on-task behavior.

Annual goals need not be written for all possible skill areas or cover the total scope of the school curriculum, but they must address areas of special concern for the particular child. Many of the educational goals for the classroom in general will also be appropriate for the mildly handicapped child. In this case, all children will have the same general goal, such as being able to read the sight words in the 4.0 grade level reader. Only when the skills of the mildly handicapped child are substantially deviant from the skill range found in the regular classroom will you need to specify separate annual goals.

DETERMINING INSTRUCTIONAL SEQUENCES

After the annual goals have been clearly stated, you must select a sequence of *intermediate steps* that will lead to mastery of these goals. While many children in the regular class make academic progress when sequences have large sequential steps, or even if the steps lack apparent order, mildly handicapped children will not succeed under such conditions. For this reason, establishing a sequence of small instructional steps that logically progress to the final goal is critical when teaching the mildly handicapped child.

There are two procedures for determining instructional sequences: extracting the sequence from available commercial material or generating your own sequence.

Extracting an Instructional Sequence

Extracting an instructional sequence is particularly appropriate if you are unfamiliar with the academic area, if you have well-sequenced material that you would like to use as the basis for your instruction, or if you would like the child to use regular classroom materials. Using sequences from commercial material is also an efficient use of teacher time. Authors have spent a great deal of time and expertise in designing instructional sequences. Why duplicate their efforts? Even if you are not satisfied with the commercial sequence as is, you can still extract a sequence and modify it for your own purposes within the classroom. (Modification is discussed more fully on page 86.)

When extracting the sequential steps, clearly state your annual goal (e.g. to use correct punctuation). Next, list the behaviors or tasks necessary to achieve that goal in order from the least complex to most complex. Then review the steps to make sure they are small enough to ensure success for mildly handicapped students. Finally, you must determine the entry skills, those behaviors needed before the student begins the first step in the sequence.

Entry behaviors were determined by asking questions concerning the sequence: What must the child know before using this instructional material? What skills does the material assume that the child has? Entry behaviors are generated both from the *demands of the skill* being taught (e.g., time telling to the minute) and the *demands of the teaching procedures* and practice activities used. The entry behaviors in Table 6.2 were determined for this time-telling sequence:

Selecting a Sequence

With the procedures outlined above clearly in mind, the teacher should consider many factors when extracting an instructional sequence. The guidelines in Table 6.2 should be followed when choosing between predetermined sequences found in commercial materials and teacher resource materials, and when evaluating a teacher-generated sequence. In selecting a sequence also consider an individual child's needs. Does the sequence match the entry behaviors of the specific child? Does the sequence lead to the annual goal determined for the child? Does the sequence consider the individual difficulties the child has in learning a new skill?

TABLE 6.2
Determining Necessary Entry Behaviors

Entry Behavior Needed	Why Necessary?
Can write numerals to 59	Necessary for writing times in programmed workbook
Can read numerals to 59	Necessary for reading of times during instructional lessons
Can discriminate between terms "long" and "short"	Necessary for discrimination of long and short hands
Can sequentially count to 60	Necessary for determining minutes. (Child does not need to count by 5's. Instruction is provided on this skill within the material.)
Can form a circle	Child circles correct responses in programmed book

TABLE 6.3
Guidelines in Selecting a Teaching Sequence

Critical questions during selection or evaluation of a teaching sequence:

1. Is the sentence written in terms of a child's behavior?

2. Does the sequence move from least complex to most complex tasks?

3. Does the sequence move from most frequent elements to least frequent elements?

4. Does the sequence include all the *enroute behaviors* that lead to the annual goal?

5. Does the sequence include a sufficient breakdown of steps for the mildly handicapped learner?

6. Does the sequence note entry skills?

7. Does the sequence group together similiar elements where it would facilitate generalization? (e.g., are short vowels taught in close proximity?)

8. If discrimination between elements is difficult, does the sequence separate them? (e.g., b from d, /ĭ/ from /ĕ/.)

9. Does the sequence gradually build on past learning?

Evaluating a sequence

Within regular education, many children can handle very large teaching steps in the teaching sequence. However, the *same* sequences may increase learning problems in handicapped children, especially when they are learning fundamental academic skills. Sequences that proceed in small, logical, easy-to-attain steps are generally the best for the handicapped learner. The *use of small sequential steps* not only ensures that the learner has mastered the necessary information for subsequent steps in the sequence, but also increases the learner's feelings of progress. If the steps are later found to be too small, they may be combined for a particular learner.

In addition to providing control in the logical ordering of small steps, the material should attempt to *teach the least complex skills and concepts before progressing to the more complex skills*. For example, in teaching phonics, single letter graphemes would be less complex than multi-letter graphemes (e.g., *l* is less complex than *fl* or *bl*). Other factors also affect the complexity of phonic elements: the number of sounds (phonemes) that a grapheme has, the number of different graphemes that represent the same sound, and the closeness of visual or auditory discrimination with other items. All skill areas have degrees of complexity that should be controlled. For example, in teaching writing, the instructor must consider that the complexity of manuscript letters depends on the number of strokes in the letter, the starting place of the letter (on a line or not), and the position of the letter in relationship to the lines. These factors should be considered when establishing the instructional sequence. Let it be stressed again that the sequence should have a definite progression from least complex to most complex.

Complexity, however, is not the sole criterion for evaluating a sequence. Though we would like children to initially learn skills that are less complex, *frequency of use* must be coupled with complexity in determining the order of a sequence. For example, if you were teaching a child the sounds of certain consonants, you would want to introduce consonants that had immediate usefulness in decoding. Consonants such as *j, w, q,* and *y* occur very infrequently in our written language and should be taught later in the instructional sequence.

Other factors also facilitate learning in the handicapped child. As much as possible, *steps in a sequence should build on past skills* that have been introduced to the child. If the child has been introduced to a number of consonants, these consonants should be used in the decoding of single vowel words as quickly as possible. When a child has learned a math skill such as place value, it should serve as the basis of instruction on regrouping in addition and subtraction. This cumulative instructional design allows the child to use past information in new learning and also facilitates continuous maintenance and review of previously introduced skills.

The *proximity of skills* in the instructional sequence must also be considered. If certain skills or concepts are placed in very close proximity, they may actually interfere with learning of the next skill. This is usually due to similar features that make it difficult to discriminate between the items. For example, the letters *b* and *d* are very similar in configuration. Placement of *d* near *b* in the sequence is likely to complicate the learning of both letters. Separation in time and practice allows the child to master one skill before being introduced to another similiar skill.

In other cases, the similarity between items actually facilitates learning and generalization between skills. A sequence should attempt to group in close proximity items whose similarities would facilitate, not interfere with, learning. For example, when learning to decode words with a final *e* and the vowel/$\bar{a}$/ (e.g., bake, rate), the student is learning a great deal about decoding of other consonant-vowel-consonant-e (CVCe) words (e.g., the sequential pronunciation of phonemes, the blending of phonemes together, and the rule governing pronunciation of vowels in this configuration). This information would certainly generalize to the decoding of other CVCe words with long vowels. To assist in this generalization, words with similar configurations should be included in close proximity within the sequence. Another example can be drawn from the area of cursive handwriting. Many of the cursive letters have the same starting place and initial stroke. When a child has learned to form the letter $\boldsymbol{e}$, she has already learned a great deal of information that she can transfer to the formation of letters $\boldsymbol{f}$, $\boldsymbol{l}$, and $\boldsymbol{h}$. To assist in the generalization, letters with similar strokes, alignment, and starting place should be taught in succession.

Modification of the Instructional Sequence

Total reorganization of the instructional sequence is often not feasible even when it appears desirable. This is particularly true when the material uses a cumulative sequence, building on previously taught skills, or continuously reviewing and maintaining skills. Many of the factors considered in the initial evaluation and selection of sequences cannot be altered when we use the material without destroying its design.

Two modifications that do not result in reordering of sequential steps are possible after the selection of materials: (1) filling in any gaps in the instructional sequence, and (2) breaking steps down into smaller steps. Let's look at an example taken from a math series:

Can solve problems involving addition of 2 digits plus 2 digits with regrouping

Can solve problems involving addition of 3 digits plus 3 digits with regrouping

Can solve problems involving addition of 4 digits plus 4 digits with regrouping

What is wrong with this sequence? Many problem types are missing. Because many handicapped children could not proceed at this rapid pace through addition with regrouping, more steps need to be provided to fill the gaps. The following steps might be added:

2 digit + 2 digit problems with regrouping
   3 digit + 1 digit problems with regrouping
   3 digit + 2 digit problems with regrouping

3 digit + 3 digit problems with regrouping
   4 digit + 1 digit problems with regrouping
   4 digit + 2 digit problems with regrouping
   4 digit + 3 digit problems with regrouping
4 digit + 4 digit problems with regrouping

Writing Your Own Sequence

Occasionally you may not be able to find a satisfactory sequence within commercial materials or other reference sources. When this happens, you can write your own sequence of instructional steps. As with sequence extraction, you must begin with an annual goal. However, before you can establish a series of steps leading to the annual goal, you first need to analyze the skill area and determine the component skills. This process is referred to as *task analysis*. Once you determine the component behaviors, you can order them from least complex to most complex, and from most frequently used skills to those that are least frequent. You will also need to determine the necessary entry behaviors for your skill sequence.

When writing sequences for academic skills, you need to consider the nature of the skill area. In a number of areas, such as multiplication operations or rote counting, there is a very natural progression of skills. These skill areas will be referred to as *developmental* to designate a fairly set ordering of steps. However, most academic areas consist of a group of related skills in which no natural sequence is evident. In these *nondevelopmental* skill areas, logical ordering is necessary to produce the best sequence for handicapped children.

Determining teaching sequences for developmental skills

A developmental skill sequence is one in which a gradual progression of steps is built on previously acquired skills. Each step is prerequisite to the next step. Examples of these skills are addition, subtraction, multiplication, and division operations. In these examples, a definite progression of skills occurs when variables are altered to increase skill difficulty. In determining the teaching sequence for this type of skill

TABLE 6.4

Sequence for Addition Operations

Annual Goal: The child will be able to perform addition operations with regrouping through four digits.

Entering Behaviors: Writes numbers to 1000. Reads numbers to 1000. Solves addition facts with sums up to 18.

2 digit plus 1 digit, no regrouping
2 digit plus 2 digit, no regrouping
3 digit plus 1 digit, no regrouping
3 digit plus 2 digit, no regrouping
3 digit plus 3 digit, no regrouping
addition of 3, 1 digit, no regrouping
addition of 4, 1 digit, no regrouping
2 digit plus 1 digit, regroup to the tens
2 digit plus 1 digit, regroup to tens and hundreds
2 digit plus 2 digit, regroup to the tens
2 digit plus 2 digit, regroup to the hundreds
2 digit plus 2 digit, regroup to tens and hundreds
3 digit plus 1 digit, regroup to tens
3 digit plus 1 digit, regroup to tens and hundreds
3 digit plus 2 digit, regroup to tens
3 digit plus 2 digit, regroup to hundreds
3 digit plus 2 digit, regroup to thousands
3 digit plus 2 digit, regroup to tens, hundreds, thousands
3 digit plus 3 digit, regroup to tens
3 digit plus 3 digit, regroup to hundreds
3 digit plus 3 digit, regroup to thousands
3 digit plus 3 digit, regroup to tens, hundreds, thousands
addition of 3, 1 digit, regroup
addition of 4, 1 digit, regroup
addition of 3, 2 digit, no regrouping
addition of 4, 2 digit, no regrouping
addition of 3, 3 digit, no regrouping
addition of 4, 3 digit, no regrouping
addition of 3, varying digits, no regrouping
addition of 3, 2 digit, regrouping
addition of 4, 2 digit, regrouping
addition of 3, 3 digit, regrouping
addition of 4, 3 digit, regrouping
addition of 3, with varying digits, regrouping

area, the question, "What makes the problems or tasks more and more difficult?" is the first step of sequencing.

You must first determine what variables can be altered to increase skill difficulty. For example, in addition computations the number of digits, the number of columns, and the inclusion of regrouping increase computation difficulty. In division, difficulty of the task is increased by the number of digits in the divisor, the number of digits in the dividend, the number of subtractions needed to complete the problem, and the inclusion of a remainder. In a visual discrimination task involving short words, the task difficulty is increased by the number of distractors present (possible alternate word choices), the length of the words, and the similarity between the words. After you have determined the crucial variables, you systematically alter them to increase problem difficulty. For example, in addition problems you might begin with addition demanding no regrouping and gradually increase the number of digits in the addends. Next you would include the variable of regrouping in problems with the fewest number of digits. You would then increase the number of digits in the addends and the complexity of regrouping. This systematic alteration of computation difficulty continues until the annual goal is met (see tables 6.4 and 6.5).

TABLE 6.5

Sequence for Matching Letters and Letter Combinations

Annual Goal: When given three similar words (three letter words), the child will consistently select the word that matches the model.

1. Matches letter to letter (one distinct distractor)—m: m t

2. Matches letter to letter (one similar distractor)—m: o m

3. Matches letter to letter (one very similar distractor)—m: m n

4. Matches letter to letter (two distinct distractors)—m: t m p

5. Matches letter to letter (two similar distractors)—m: m r h

6. Matches letter to letter (two very similar distractors)—m: n m r

7. (Repeat with three distractors.)

8. Matches letter pair to letter pair (one distinct distractor)—to: ij to

9. Matches letter pair to letter pair (one similar distractor)—to: to le

10. Matches letter pair to letter pair (one very similar distractor)—to: lo to

11. Matches letter pair to letter pair (two distinct distractors)—re: re jo il

12. Matches letter pair to letter pair (two similar distractors)—re: no re ri

13. Matches letter pair to letter pair (two very similar distractors)—re: re ne ra

Continue pattern.

NOTE: Matching words with varied length. The teacher first determined the variables that could be altered to increase task difficulty. Variables included length of the words, number of distractors (possible alternate word choices) present, and the similarity between the distractors and the model.

Determining teaching sequence for nondevelopmental skills

In some academic skill areas there are a number of related component elements that do not have a natural sequential order; that is, the mastery of a certain element is not necessarily a prerequisite to mastery of the other elements. For example, you may wish to teach a child to name the shapes of a circle, a square, a triangle, and a rectangle. Though there is probably some difference in skill difficulty between the shapes, the child could learn the names of the shapes in any order. The naming of the circle is not a necessary prerequisite to naming any of the other shapes. In this case you must determine: (1) the *related elements* included in the skill areas, (2) the *order* of the elements, and finally, (3) the *steps* to be used in teaching each of the related elements. Because the elements are often similar, the same sequential teaching steps can be used for each one.

Step one: Specify Component Elements. After determining the annual goal, you will then specify the component elements to be taught under the related skill area. You might determine the elements by using a "shot gun method"—simply writing down all elements that you would cover under a specific skill area. This can also be done by brainstorming with another person. For example, if the goal is, "Sally will be able to decode words with short vowels in the CVC configuration," the component elements would include the vowels *a, e, i, o,* and *u*. Or, if the goal is learning the use of punctuation marks, the teacher begins the process of sequencing by listing the component elements to be taught: period, question mark, exclamation point, comma, and quotation mark. If you are not well versed in a skill area, you could look at established material to determine elements often defined under the areas in which you feel deficient.

Step two: Order Elements. After you determine component elements, order them for instruction. Because these skill areas are not developmental in nature, their sequence is more arbitrary. However, the evaluation guidelines for sequences presented earlier in the chapter can be used to determine the ordering of elements in a related skill sequence. Though there may be little divergence of difficulty between them, the order should begin with the least complex and move to the most complex. For example, after you list all of the phonetic elements to be taught, reorder them so that the consonants occur before the short vowels. (Do this because of the higher consistency of the consonant sounds over the vowel sounds.) You should also order the elements by frequency of occurrence so that ones that occur more frequently are taught first. For example, the common inflectional endings *s, ed,* and *ing* occur more often and should be taught before the less frequent elements *est* and *er*. In the same way, short vowels should be introduced before vowel diphthongs and digraphs because they occur more frequently in words.

As we have emphasized before, in ordering the elements, you will wish to group them if their similarity might assist in acquisition of each separate one. For example, long *a, i, o,* and *u* in the CVCe configuration might be taught in successive order because the learning of one configuration could reduce the amount of time needed for the acquisition of a similar element. Occasionally, however, elements in a related skill area will have characteristics that interfere with the learning of other elements. This is particularly true when the discrimination between the elements is very similar and can create difficulty in learning later items. If this occurs, elements should be separated in the instructional sequence. For example, many children may have difficulty discriminating among the written letters *b, p,* and *d.* It is helpful that the letters be separated in the sequence to their phoneme-grapheme relations.

Step three: Determine Steps to Teach Elements. It is not enough to order the elements logically; you must now decide what steps will be used in teaching each of them. Again, draw on your own knowledge of teaching an element, or draw on commercial materials or teacher reference books for delineation of steps. If the elements included in the sequence are closely related, the steps used for teaching one item can also be used for teaching other items. For example, after you order all the phonetic elements, determine the following steps for teaching each of them:

1. Associates the phoneme with the grapheme (e.g., says phoneme when given grapheme)

2. Decodes words with the element

3. Decodes words with the element in the context of phrases and sentences.

Then repeat these successive steps in introducing each of the elements. Examples of teaching sequences for nondevelopmental skills are found in tables 6.6, 6.7, and 6.8.

TABLE 6.6

Sequence for Lowercase Letters

Long-term Objective: When given the verbal name of each alphabet letter, Harry will be able to correctly reproduce each letter without a model, with correct alignment, size and height.

Entry Behaviors: Holds a pencil. Scribbles freely on paper. Discriminates letter forms when similar distractors are present. Traces a model of a vertical line, a horizontal line, a slanted line and a circle. Copies a model of the above forms. On verbal command, draws a "line down," a "line across," and a "circle."

Elements: Though each will be taught separately, the elements have been grouped to stress similarity between strokes. This sequence was developed by grouping letters with the same strokes or combination of strokes.

Group 1: Straight line letters: $(l\ t\ i\ )$

Group 2: Straight and slant line letters: $(v\ x\ w y\ z\ )$

Group 3: Circle and curve letters: $(o\ c\ s)$

Group 4: Circle and line letters: $(a\ b\ e\ p\ i\ g\ d\ q\ )$

Curve and line letters: $(h\ m\ k\ n\ f\ r\ u)$

Steps for teaching each letter formation during initial acquisition:

Step 1. Child can trace a letter
   with solid line: $+\ +\ +\ +\ +\ +$
   with faded line:
   with dotted line:

Step 2. Child can copy a letter to model
   with model and starting point given:

TABLE 6.6 *Sequence for Lowercase Letters (con't)*

with model given: ___+|_____

with model exposed and quickly removed (flash card): ___[t]_____

Step 3. Child can write a letter to a verbal cue: ___+_____

NOTE: In establishing this sequence to teach the writing of lowercase manuscript writing, the teacher decided to group the words by strokes or combination of strokes. Although there are many options in establishing a skill sequence, the sequence should be selected to meet the individual student's needs. For this reason another teacher might select to present the letters in alphabetic order and to simultaneously teach the child how to name and write the letters. For another child, the teacher might wish to separate the letters with similar configuration because of the child's difficulty with visual discrimination.

TABLE 6.7

Sequence for Drawing Shapes   ART 13

Annual goal: Child will be able to reproduce all basic shapes without a model present.

Entering Behaviors: Child knows how to match, identify and name the basic shapes.

Elements: 1. circle   3. triangle
             2. square   4. rectangle

Teaching steps to be used with each element:

1. Trace the shape with a template or other device given starting point

2. Trace the shape with no device and a starting point

3. Trace the shape with a solid line and no starting point

4. Trace the shape with a dotted line and a starting point

5. Trace the shape with a dotted line and no starting point

6. Copy a shape to model when starting point is given

TABLE 6.7 *Sequence for Drawing Shapes (con't)*

7. Copy a shape to model when starting point is not given

8. Draw a shape when no model is given

NOTE: In this sequence the teacher first determined what elements she wished to teach. The teacher then determined the steps she would use in teaching the elements. She asked herself, "How can I systematically increase the difficulty of the task? What enroute behaviors would the child need to perform before drawing the shape with no model?" Though all children would not need this many steps to master the terminal goal, by writing down a very finely developed sequence the teacher has an outline of steps for the child who is having extreme difficulty with the task.

TABLE 6.8

Sequence for Direction Following

Annual goal: When given directional words, *circle, check, underline,* and *put an X on* and *cross out,* Sally will be able to follow two directions given at the same time on a worksheet.

Elements: Selected because of their high use on workbook assignments in the class.

1. (Circle)   4. Cross out
2. Check ✓   5. Put an X on ✗
3. Underline

Teaching steps for all elements:

1. Can follow one direction for one stimuli when given two choices.
   Example: Circle the flower.

2. Can follow one direction for one stimuli when given three choices.
   Example: Circle the tree.

3. Can follow one direction for one stimuli when given four choices.
   Example: Circle the cat.

TABLE 6.8 *Sequence for Direction following (con't)*

    4. Can follow one direction for one stimuli when given five choices.
       Example: Circle the flower.

    5. Can follow one direction word for two stimuli when given three choices.
       Example: Circle the flower and the tree.

    6. Can follow one direction for two stimuli when four choices are given.
       Example: Circle the tree and the cat.

Teaching steps when all elements have been mastered for above steps:

    1. Can follow one direction for one stimuli when given two choices and direction
       words are altered throughout the exercise.
       Example: Circle the square:

       Circle the tree:

    2. Can follow one direction for one stimulus when given three choices and direction
       words are altered throughout the exercise.
       Example: Circle the box:

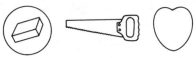

       Underline the heart:

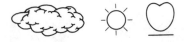

TABLE 6.8 *Sequence for Direction Following (con't)*

3. Can follow one direction for one stimulus when given four choices and direction words are altered throughout the exercise.

   Example: Circle the top:

   Cross out the flower:

4. Can follow one direction for two stimuli when given three choices and direction words are altered throughout the exercise.

   Example: Underline the house and the man:

   Cross out the tree and the flower:

Teaching steps when all elements have been mastered for above steps: (cont.)

5. Can follow one direction for two stimuli when given four choices and direction words are altered throughout the exercise.

   Example: Circle the dog and the tree:

   Underline the orange and the apple:

6. Can follow two directions given at the same time when four choices and direction are varied in the exercise.

   Example: Circle the dog and cross out the cat:

TABLE 6.8 *Sequence for Direction Following (con't)*

Underline the tree and put an X on the house:

NOTE: In this sequence the teacher developed a sequence for teaching primary direction-following for a child having difficulty following the common classroom directions needed in order to complete kindergarten and first grade level paper-and-pencil tasks. The teacher first determined the direction words to teach and then determined the developmental steps for each of the direction words. The steps for proficiency using a mixture of directions were then determined.

Translating Sequence Steps into Short-Term Objectives

To meet the requirements of an IEP, you will need to write the sequential steps as short-term objectives. Short-term objectives not only include the desired behavior, but also designate the learner, the conditions under which the behavior will be measured, and the criterion used to determine mastery and subsequent movement to a new short-term objective. Short-term objectives provide additional direction and guidance to the teacher, who now knows what should be taught, how the skill will be measured, and what level of performance is expected. For example, one of the steps in the time-telling sequence is "will be able to tell time to the minute." Though this is quite specific, it does not provide Molly's teacher with information on how the skill will be measured or the desired performance criterion. If these were added, the short-term objective might read like this:

> When given a real clock set to the hour and minute, Molly will say the time, including the hour and minute, correctly in 9 out of 10 trials.

Behavioral objectives always include *who* is doing *what* under what *conditions* and to what *criterion*, and are usually written in the following standard format:

conditions   *who*   *what*

When given a sheet of CVC words with short vowel *i*, Molly will orally read the

criterion

words at a rate of 45 per minute with not more than two errors.

See Table 6.9 for a sequence of short-term objectives written in this standard form. Although short-term objectives should include these components, many busy teachers use abbreviated forms for objectives. You may even wish to use a table format to simplify the process. The formats in Tables 6.10, 6.11 and 6.12 illustrate possible abbreviated forms which include all the necessary elements for complete short-term objectives (the "enroute" steps in a sequence).

TABLE 6.9

Standard Form for Short-term Objectives

Annual Goal:	When given a verbal or written cue, Molly can select from a group of coins exact amounts with values up to $1.00.
Entry behaviors:	Can name coins Can tell the value of the coin

TABLE 6.9 *Standard Forms for Short-term Objectives (con't)*

Can give common equivalents for coins (e.g., two dimes and a nickel for a quarter)

Can count by 1s, 5s, 10s and 25s (Could be taught within sequence)

Coin Counting—All Same Coin

When given a set of pennies with values from 2¢ to 50¢, Molly will be able to count the coins and say the value with 100% accuracy.

When given a set of nickels with values from 10¢ to $1.00, Molly will be able to count the coins and say the value with 100% accuracy.

When given a set of dimes with values from 20¢ to $1.00, Molly will be able to count the coins and say the value with 100% accuracy.

When given a set of quarters with values from 50¢ to $1.00, Molly will be able to count the coins and say the value with 100% accuracy.

When given two half dollars, Molly will be able to count the coins and say the value with 100% accuracy.

When given a group of pennies, Molly will be able to select out a value less than the total value (e.g., 31¢, 16¢) with 100% accuracy.

When given a group of nickels, Molly will be able to select out a value less than the total value with 100% accuracy.

When given a group of dimes, Molly will be able to select out a value less than the total value with 100% accuracy.

When given a group of quarters, Molly will be able to select out a value less than the total value with 100% accuracy.

When given a group of half dollars, Molly will be able to select out a value less than the total value with 100% accuracy.

Coin Counting—Different coins

When given a set of different coins with value to 10¢, Molly will be able to count the coins and say the value with 100% accuracy.

Continue same objective for values to: 25¢   (Child should begin counting
                                         50¢   with the largest coin.)
                                         75¢
                                         99¢

When given a group of different coins, Molly will be able to select out a value less than the total value to 10¢ with 100% accuracy.

Continue same objective for values to: 25¢
                                         50¢
                                         75¢
                                         99¢

NOTE: This sequence begins with counting same coins and continues through counting and selecting different coins to match a specific value.

TABLE 6.10

Abbreviated Forms of Short-term Objectives

WHO: MOLLY

GIVEN:	10 CVC words
WILL:	write down (spell)
AT:	9 of 10 correct on 2 consecutive days

GIVEN:	sheet with 100 CVVC words on it
WILL:	read orally
AT:	50 correct words per minute, no more than 2 errors per minute

GIVEN:	sheet of 100 add facts, sums to 18
WILL:	write sums
AT:	50 correct, no more than 3 errors per minute

TABLE 6.11

Annual Goal: Given a probe sheet with CVC words with short vowels, Molly says the words.

Conditions	Behavior	Standard/criterion
CVC probe, short a	says words	45/min. 2 errors
CVC probe, short e	says words	45/min. 2 errors
CVC probe, short o	says words	45/min. 2 errors
CVC probe, short i	says words	45/min. 2 errors
CVC probe, short u	says words	45/min. 2 errors
CVC probe, mixed		
short a,e,i,o,u	says words	45/min. 2 errors

TABLE 6.12

Abbreviated Forms of Short-term Objectives

Child:	Molly
Annual Goal:	When given a list of 50 words with inflectional endings *ing, ed, s* mixed with noninflected words, Molly will read orally. (Note: roots will be known words or phonetically regular words.)

Conditions	Behavior	Criterion
When given a list of words with:	Will:	At:
ending s and all roots	read orally	95%
ending ing and unaltered roots	read orally	95%
ending ed and unaltered roots	read orally	95%

TABLE 6.12 *Abbreviated Forms of Short-term Objectives (con't)*

endings s, ing, ed, and unaltered roots	read orally	95%
endings ing and ed and roots demanding doubling of the final consonant (batting)	read orally	95%
endings ing and ed and roots final silent e	read orally	95%
ending ed with final consonant y roots (tried)	read orally	95%
ing, ed, s endings with all root types	read orally	95%

Criteria for Mastery. One of the most difficult aspects of writing short-term objectives is writing appropriate criteria on which to base movement to a new short-term objective. Though the setting of criteria is somewhat arbitrary, there are a few guidelines that you can follow. First, decide if you are interested in accuracy (stated in terms of a percentage) or rate (stated in terms of numbers correct and incorrect per minute). For many skill areas, particularly basic skill areas, such as spelling, writing a sentence, or computation, our main concern is accuracy, not rate of response. Only after a child has conquered the basics of a skill should her rate of response be emphasized.

However, for many skills, accuracy alone does not indicate proficiency. If a child decodes words with 100% accuracy but only completes five words in a minute, she would not have a functional skill. Likewise, if a child completes 25 addition facts with sums from 0 to 10 in ten minutes with no errors, this would still not reflect proficiency in addition facts. To show mastery of addition facts, the child would need to exhibit a faster rate reflecting instant recall of the sums. Because rate of response *is* important, you may wish to measure it for skill areas such as saying sounds, subtracting, oral reading in a meaning-based basal, writing cursive letters, and decoding CVVC words with long vowel digraphs. To record rate of response, you simply record the numbers of correct and incorrect responses made by the child while performing the skill for one minute. Many regular classroom teachers use rate measures with their entire class to increase motivation.

When accuracy is the criterion for mastery, you must consider how complex the skill is and how critical it is to higher level skills to determine the desired rate of mastery. With basic skills fundamental to later learning, such as solving addition facts, saying numeral names, or writing letters, you should demand a rate of 95 to 100% accuracy. These high standards will lead to overlearning through practice and drill, and will increase the probability of retention by building a firmer foundation for later skills. With complex skills such as decoding five- or six-syllable words, you should establish a lower accuracy level of 85 to 95% since even proficient learners have difficulty with such tasks.

You can use a number of procedures to determine an appropriate rate criterion for a child. It could be based on the child's own optimum rate on a similar skill. For example, John's oral reading rate in a book at his independent level (the level at which he can read comfortably without direct teacher help) could be used as an indication of a desired rate in a more difficult material.

You can also determine rate criterion from the performance of other children in your classroom. If you wish to use this procedure, ask several children in your classroom to perform a specific skill such as saying sounds, decoding words, or solving division facts. You can then use their average rate of performance along with specific information on the mildly handicapped child to establish a desired level of performance.

In all cases, your performance standard is a "best guess" that can be adjusted if found to be inappropriate for the child. Occasionally, the mildly handicapped child will not retain previously taught skills even though she mastered the desired criterion before moving to a new skill. When this happens, you may need to adjust the criterion upward or increase the number of days at the desired standard to increase the probability of overlearning and increased retention. For example, you could increase the criterion from 90% to 95% or increase the number of days at the desired standard from one day to three consecutive days. On the other hand, if a child appears very proficient at a skill but has not met the established standard, a downward adjustment can be made. The criterion, however, should not be lowered simply to speed up movement between skills. If the criterion is lowered, retention of the skill should be measured in subsequent weeks to ensure maintenance of the behavior. Establishment of appropriate criteria will be discussed in chapter 8 when data-recording systems are introduced.

7

SELECTING INSTRUCTIONAL ACTIVITIES: HOW TO TEACH

When assessment is complete and annual goals and sequential short-term objectives have been determined, instructional programming can begin. Instructional activities in the classroom can be broken down into *direct teacher instruction* and *independent practice activities*. During direct teacher instruction the teacher instructs the child how to perform skills or teaches him new concepts. In addition, the teacher supervises practice of the new skill or concept and provides feedback on the student's performance. Independent practice activities are those classroom activities that are independently completed by the child. In the past, these activities have been referred to as seatwork. However, they can go beyond paper and pencil tasks completed at the child's desk to include any activity the child performs without the direct interaction of the teacher, such as work with instructional media or completion of projects. Independent practice activities must be carefully planned so that you are free to work with individual children or small groups as well as provide the children with the opportunity to practice a new skill.

In acquiring a new skill or concept, a child progresses through the three stages of learning: *initial acquisition, proficiency,* and *maintenance.* During the stage of initial acquisition, the child is told how to perform the desired behavior, and learns minimal usage of the skill. She then moves to the second stage in which she improves her accuracy and rate of performance on a skill. The short-term objective should include a criterion of mastery that indicates when a child has reached a desired level of proficiency. When the child becomes proficient in the skill, practice is required for maintenance of the desired level of performance. Some skills are maintained by

Anita Archer

the performance of higher level skills (e.g., two-place multiplication maintains multiplication facts), while other skills need an organized system of review within the classroom.

It is helpful to examine, these stages of learning in relationship to *direct teacher instruction* and *independent child activities.*

DIRECT TEACHER INSTRUCTION

One of the major tenets in education of the mildly handicapped has been individualization. Annual goals and short-term objectives, pace in materials, and practice activities, have all been individualized. But although considerations of individual needs, entry behaviors, and movement through an instructional sequence have validity in teaching mildly handicapped children, individualization has all too often been merely a child working alone, working in materials without direct teacher instruction, and completing individual ditto pages in a folder. But because of their special needs, mildly handicapped children require more, not less, direct teacher instruction. Learning as a result of this interaction with the teacher is much more likely to improve children's academic skills than any amount of independent folder work.

Even though PL 94-142 calls for individualized educational programs, it does not require that the mildly handicapped child be taught on a one-to-one basis. One-to-one instruction, while having the most potential for individualization, is not the most efficient use of teacher time. Indeed, if all children had to be instructed individually, the teacher would actually have very little time to devote to any single child. Of course, when a child's skills differ substantially from those of his peers, one-to-one instruction can be used, particularly through the use of volunteers, peer tutors, and older tutors. However, a more practical method of teaching is small-group instruction. It allows the teacher to instruct more than one child at a time, but still allows for individual responses and teacher feedback on child performance in a way that large- or whole-group instruction does not. Whole-group instruction may be appropriate for other subject areas such as history, social studies, science, art, music, current events, physical education, and health.

With the focus narrowed to one-to-one or small-group instruction on basic academic subjects, you can analyze and evaluate direct instructional activities presented in materials as well as formulate your own direct instructional activities. Teachers instruct students by presenting new skills and concepts, attending to children's responses and feeding back to children the results of their performance.

Presentation of Skills and Concepts

If you expect a child to acquire a skill and concept, you must teach the skill directly through the use of *verbal instruction, modeling* (showing the desired skill followed by child imitation), and/or *demonstration* or *physical guidance.* These activities are the foundation of all teaching. When using verbal instruction to present a concept or describe how to perform a skill, the teacher must speak precisely and present the information in an organized, step-by-step manner. For example, if the teacher is describing how to make a cursive letter, he might say, "We are going to make the letter ♪. We begin at the baseline. Come up to the midline, around and back to the baseline and finish." As the teacher describes how to make the cursive letter, he would also demonstrate the letter formation on an overhead projector or on a chalkboard and then ask the child to imitate or model his performance. The following guidelines are particularly helpful in presenting information and skills to the mildly handicapped children in your classroom.

Be sure the child is attentive during direct teacher instruction

During small-group or individual instruction, you can improve the children's attention by arranging their chairs so each child can see you and the stimuli used during instruction. A semi-circle arrangement of chairs whereby you can be seated in the center is often effective. You might even organize the desks permanently into groupings so that all children can see during small-group instruction (table 7.1).

TABLE 7.1

Physical Arrangement for Small-Group Instruction

Semi-circle reading table

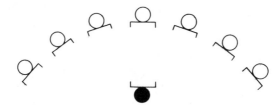

Semi-circle arrangement of chairs around teacher

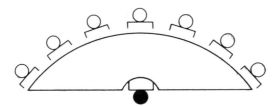

Semi-circle arrangement of children on rug or floor

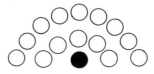

Horseshoe arrangement of children in chairs around teacher

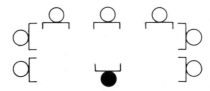

TABLE 7.1 *Physical Arrangement for Small-Group Instruction (cont.)*

Permanent arrangement of desks in small groupings that can be used for instruction

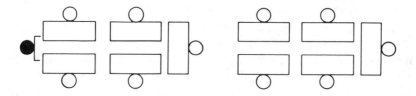

Permanent groupings of desks that can be used for small group instruction

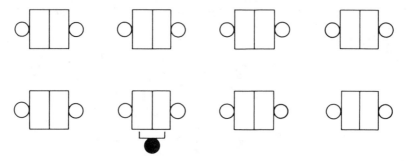

Children with fewer skills or lower ability in the particular subject should be placed in the center of the group. There, the lower-performing children will be closer to you and will be surrounded by attending children. The children who are having greatest difficulty often select the most distant chair to avoid participation; as a result, they gain the least during instructional periods. Be aware of this behavior and continually draw the child into the instructional activities.

You can also use *cueing words* such as *listen now, look* and *ready* to establish and maintain attentive behavior. Gestures such as a raised hand, a finger pointing at an important stimulus, or a beckoning gesture can also be used to increase attention. Often you can pair verbal and gestural cues; you might say *look here* and point to the word on the board. These attending cues are most effective when consistently used with a group of children, so that the children will begin to associate the desired behavior with the cues that you give.

Directly teach the desired skill

If you are to teach the mildly handicapped child efficiently and systematically, your instruction must be directly related to the desired outcome behavior. If you want a child to correctly spell the word *want*, spelling instruction must be directly related to the sequence of the letters in *want*. For instance, you might say: "This word is *want*. What is this word? Listen to me spell *want*, W-A-N-T. Touch each letter and spell it with me. W-A-N-T. What word? Good, this is the word *want*, W A N T. Cover up *want* and write it." Verbal instruction and demonstration of the correct spelling were used in presenting the word. Other types of instructional activities (e.g., saying the word in a sentence, discussing the meaning of *want*, looking at the configuration of *want*) would be less direct and would have less potential for teaching this particular skill.

Other examples are more obvious. Early readiness materials often use tasks and instruction that are only remotely related to the desired skills. For example, activities such as discriminating between people's voices, discriminating between the sounds of objects, and repeating pencil taps on a desk are often suggested when the real goal is auditory discrimination of initial phonemes (sounds) in words. If you wish a child to acquire a skill, your instruction must address that skill directly.

Many instructional lessons use discovery approaches, in which the child is to discover generalizations or concepts either through incidental or systematic presentation of stimuli. Whether a discovery or "telling" approach is used with mildly handicapped children, the process should not be incidental but systematic. The mildly handicapped child cannot afford to misinterpret or fail to acquire the expected information. To ensure that the handicapped child has mastered the information, it is often helpful to follow up discovery lessons with more direct telling of the concept or skill.

Break instruction down into small, logical steps

We thoroughly discussed the importance of a step-by-step instructional sequence in Chapter 6, but let us reiterate that this is one of the most necessary guidelines to follow in teaching the mildly handicapped child.

Use visual stimuli in addition to verbal instruction

Children process information not only auditorily but also visually. In fact, some children have more success in processing visual information. For this reason, it is often helpful to provide visual materials and stimuli (gesture cues, tracing letters in the air) during verbal instruction on a new skill or task. Visual stimuli not only increase the probability that the child will attend to the direct teacher instruction, but may also increase the ease of acquiring the new skill. Some skills such as map reading cannot be presented without the appropriate visual stimuli. However, visual stimuli can be adapted to instruction in all skills. The teacher can present actual objects, pictures, or representations on the board, overhead projector, tagboard cards, or tagboard strips. For example, in teaching the use of direct quotation marks to set off the exact words of the speaker, presentation of written examples with quotation marks are more effective then verbal explanations only. Sometimes visual aids may be used in a non-traditional manner. For example, a child might have difficulty in the auditory discrimination of a medial vowel sound. To help the child focus on the correct medial, you might use a visual display of three lines: __ __ __. As the child stretched out the word in order to listen to the medial sound, he would point to the three lines: *c, a, t,* thus identifying the medial sound as he pointed to the middle line.

Child Responses and Practice

Another important aspect of direct teacher instruction is the use of child responses and practice which serve many valuable purposes: (1) active involvement increases attention; (2) intermittent child responses force the teacher to present information in a more logical fashion; (3) child responses provide feedback to the teacher on the success of her teaching; (4) child responses verify that they understand the information taught in class; (5) practice is increased; and (6) teacher feedback and corrections are possible on child responses. The value of active child responses and practice during instruction can be increased by the following procedures.

Provide instruction before demanding child responses

In many classes, the teacher will ask the following types of questions at the beginning of a lesson: "Who can tell me the sound of *oi*?" or "Who can show us how to add these numbers?" The teacher waits for a response from a "knowing" child. After listening to the child's responses, the teacher reinforces the child for her answer. A number of things have happened in this exchange: (1) because the teacher has heard from only one child with the skill, she may be misled concerning the group's skill in this area.; (2) the child who had already mastered the skill receives additional practice while those who may lack the skill receive less practice; (3) the teacher reinforces the child who already possesses the skill and does not reinforce new learning or attending to new information. To avoid this trap, the teacher is wise to present information *before* eliciting child responses. The value of the child responses is greatly increased when they follow direct instruction on which the responses are based. In this way, all children can potentially respond, practice can be provided for *all* learners, and the responses provide the teacher with better feedback on the learners' skill acquisition and the impact of the skill presentation.

Attempt to reduce errors

When children are first practicing skills or responding to instruction, it is important for their responses to be relatively error free. If a child practices an error or an error pattern, learning of the skill or concept correctly will be more difficult. The teacher can do a number of things to reduce the probability of error. For example, she can present information systematically and logically before demanding a child response. Errors are less likely to occur when the desired task is made very clear and the teacher provides a prompt or cue to assist the children in initial performance of the skill.

Using Visual Prompts to Reduce Errors. In using visual prompts, you give the child a partial answer. For example, you might highlight short vowel words with the CVC configuration with color to remind the child of the appropriate sounds. When giving instruction on cursive letters, you might provide initial practice in forming letters with slashed lines, and later give the child dotted lines to follow. When teaching the use of punctuation in a sentence, you could cue the appropriate placement of punctuation by leaving a box for each punctuation mark needed. Visual prompts are also very helpful when teaching a child complex math operations. You can add lines and arrows to cue the child on the correct placement of numbers. Visual prompts may be of assistance when a child is beginning to practice a spelling word; you might indicate the number of letters needed with dashed lines. Visual prompts should be faded as soon as the child increases her proficiency and can perform the task independently. Many times you should gradually reduce the prompts rather than eliminate them altogether, so that the child is performing with more and more independence (see tables 7.2, 7.3, and 7.4).

TABLE 7.2

Use of Visual Prompts in Teaching Math Operations

Faded visual prompts in the instruction of one-digit–plus–two-digit addition with carrying

$$
\begin{array}{c}
\textit{0} \\
3\ 4 \\
+\quad 8 \\
\hline
\end{array}
\qquad
\begin{array}{c}
0 \\
3\ 4 \\
+\quad 8 \\
\hline
\end{array}
\qquad
\begin{array}{c}
0 \\
34 \\
+\ 8 \\
\hline
\end{array}
\qquad
\begin{array}{c}
0 \\
34 \\
+\ 8 \\
\hline
\end{array}
\qquad
\begin{array}{c}
34 \\
+\ 8 \\
\hline
\end{array}
$$

Faded visual prompts used in the instruction of one-digit into two-digit division

$$
4\overline{)52} \qquad 4\overline{)52} \qquad 4\overline{)52} \qquad 4\overline{)52}
$$

Faded visual prompts used in the instruction of one-digit–times–two-digit multiplication

$$
\begin{array}{c}
0 \\
4\ 2. \\
\times\ 7 \\
\hline
\end{array}
\qquad
\begin{array}{c}
4\ 2 \\
\times\ 7 \\
\hline
\end{array}
\qquad
\begin{array}{c}
42 \\
\times\ 7 \\
\hline
\end{array}
\qquad
\begin{array}{c}
42 \\
\times\ 7 \\
\hline
\end{array}
\qquad
\begin{array}{c}
42 \\
\times\ 7 \\
\hline
\end{array}
$$

Faded visual prompts used in the instruction of two-digit multiplication

$$
\begin{array}{c}
32 \\
\times\ 24 \\
\hline
+ \\
\hline
\end{array}
\qquad
\begin{array}{c}
32 \\
\times\ 24 \\
\hline
\end{array}
\qquad
\begin{array}{c}
32 \\
\times\ 24 \\
\hline
\end{array}
\qquad
\begin{array}{c}
32 \\
\times\ 24 \\
\hline
\end{array}
$$

TABLE 7.3

Use of Visual Prompts in Teaching Handwriting

Faded visual prompts in the instruction of cursive letter formation

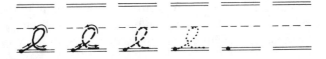

TABLE 7.3 *Use of Visual Prompts in Teaching Handwriting (cont.)*

Faded visual prompts in the instruction of manuscript letter formation

Additional visual cueing devices used in the instruction of handwriting

Directional arrows:

Colored start and stop points for each stroke:
  o red   *x* green

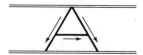

Colored-coded baseline and top line:
          red
          _____

          _ _ _ _ _ _ _ _ _ _ _ _

        green
Heavy-lined baseline:

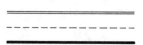

Pale vertical lines (or sheet with vertical lines placed under handwriting sheet):

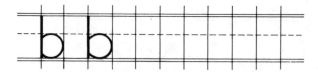

Using Verbal Prompts to Reduce Errors. Verbal prompts also assist the child in making the correct response when initially learning a new skill. For example, in teaching a child to form the cursive letter *t* you might use verbal prompts on the letter formation: "Ready. Up, down, around, and cross." When instructing the child to form the manuscript letter *t* you might direct the child to "touch, pull down, touch, pull across." A simple verbal reminder might be used to reduce error responses. For instance, in teaching regrouping in addition, you might remind the child, "Begin on the right side, remember to carry if the number is greater than nine." Verbal cues might also be given in decoding words. "Remember that the letters *oi*, as in the world *oil*, have the sound 'oi.' "

TABLE 7.4

Use of Visual Prompts in Teaching Decoding with
Specific Decoding Patterns

Faded visual prompts added to assist in decoding words with vowel digraphs in which phoneme is name of first vowel

boat   boat   boat

rain   rain   rain

Faded visual prompts added to assist in decoding words with vowel configuration of CVCE with final silent *e*

bake   bake   bake   bake

Verbal rules are often helpful to children when learning a new skill if carefully worded to actually guide performance of the skill and to reduce confusion in the performance of other skills. For example, in teaching math operations and handwriting, you can verbalize rules to assist the child (see tables 7.5 and 7.6).

TABLE 7.5

Use of Verbal Prompts in the Teaching of Math Operations

Verbal prompts used in the instruction of addition with regrouping

Problem type:
36	"Work from the right to the left."
+25	"Be sure to regroup when needed."

Verbal prompts used in the instruction of subtraction with regrouping

Problem type:
38	306	"Work from the right to the left."
−19	−29	"Be sure to regroup when needed."
		"Always subtract the bottom number from the top number."
		"Watch for zeros when you regroup."

Verbal prompts used in the instruction of multiplication

Problem type:
38	"Multiply by the one's column first."
×27	"Remember to line up the numbers carefully."
	"Remember to cross multiply."

TABLE 7.6

Use of Verbal Cues in the Instruction of Handwriting

Use of verbal prompts in the formation of manuscript letters. Have the child repeat the verbal directions as he forms the letters. Use consistent vocabulary. (The words *touch, pull, across,* and *around* were used in this example.)

 A: touch-pull, touch-pull, touch-across

 W: touch-pull, touch-pull, touch-pull, touch-pull

 b: touch-pull, touch-around

 c: touch-around

 f: touch-around-pull, touch-across

Use of verbal prompts in the formation of cursive letters. Use consistent vocabulary for strokes. (The words *up, down, around,* and *finish* were used here.) Be sure verbalizations fit formation of letter and stress smoothness of strokes used.

b: up, down, around, finish

a: around, down, finish

o: around, finish

f: up, down, around, and finish

Using Physical Guidance to Reduce Errors. Although fewer skills can be adapted to the use of physical guidance than to the use of visual and verbal prompts, physical guidance can be helpful in reducing errors in academic skills such as writing manuscript letters, coloring within the lines, positioning hands on a typewriter, or operating a tape recorder in the classroom. In teaching many physical education activities, physical guidance might also be used. Guidance would be appropriate when teaching ball bouncing, throwing a softball, kicking a football, or walking across a balance beam.

Provide adequate amounts of practice under supervision

Direct teacher instruction on basic academic tool subjects should never evolve as a teacher monologue. The children should be actively involved in the instruction and continually making responses. These may be group responses and/or individual responses. When using unison responses, the teacher asks for all children to respond to a direction or question. The task must be fairly simple, the teacher must clearly communicate the desired task, the response demands must be obvious, and the teacher must give a clear prompt which is followed by the unison response. Unison responses have a number of advantages: *all* children are involved, the number of active responses are increased, and the children's attention is better maintained (one's attention often wanes when listening to others responding). Individual responses are an effective follow-up of unison responses and provide the teacher with more accurate information on individual attainment of a skill or concept. They also allow for individual feedback or corrections.

Responses can be verbal or motoric (pointing, gesturing, writing, circling, underlining). The responses demanded of the child should be as closely related to the final skill responses as possible. For example, in spelling, written responses are more desirable than verbal ones. If the goal is for the child to solve long-division problems, actual written responses on the operations would be of more value than verbally describing the steps. Though various responses would be appropriate, the better responses are those with a reduced error potential, which follow direct instruction and require responses directly related to the desired skill performance.

Teacher feedback on child performance

Teacher feedback is another important component of this direct instructional interaction between the teacher and the learners. During direct teacher instruction, the teacher is continually eliciting child responses and providing for practice of new skills under supervision. To maximize the effectiveness of this practice, the teacher needs to provide feedback for both correct and incorrect responses. Instructional materials should delineate reinforcement and correction procedures within their lesson outlines.

Feedback and reinforcement for correct responses

To continue performing skills in a desired manner, the child must be aware of when a skill is correctly performed. Feedback can be very general and simply indicate a correct response: "Good, that is right," or "Nice job." But feedback that is paired with a "why" is even more helpful: "Nice job, you blended the sounds together quickly," or "That is just right. All the numbers in the problem are neatly lined up," or "You got all of the answers correct." In these examples, the child is reinforced for a correct response *and* receives additional feedback on exactly what was good about it.

Feedback and corrections for errors

Any corrections that follow an error should be dependent on the reason the child made an error. By analyzing the child's response, the teacher can analyze the error and follow up with an effective correction. Tables 7.7 and 7.8 list strategies for correcting errors.

TABLE 7.7

Correcting Error Responses During Direct Teacher Instruction

Cause of Error	*Hierarchy of Correction Procedures*
Child did not understand the task.	1. Repeat the task.
	2. If the child is still unable to perform the task, explain or model the task.
Child was not attending	1. Repeat the task.
	2. If the child still appears not to be attending, use some prompt to gain attention (cue word, touch, physical proximity, gesture) and then repeat task.
Child is attending and understands the task, but makes an error. Error is due to insufficient mastery of the information.	1. If the teacher has reason to believe that the child can perform the skill, the teacher can repeat the task.

TABLE 7.7 *Correcting Error Responses During Direct Teacher Instruction (cont.)*

2. If the child continues to make an error when presented with the task again, or the skill is a new one, the teacher should provide a prompt to assist the child in performing the skill (partial information on how to perform the skill).

It is helpful if you use the same correction procedure systematically for similar errors. For example, if an error is made in spelling a word, the teacher may indicate the occurence of the error and provide the same correction (e.g., presentation of the written word). In all cases, the child should make the desired correct response after the correction procedure. A specific cycle should emerge:

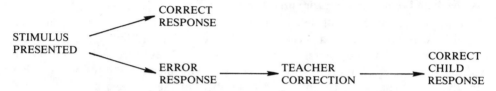

Evaluation and Modification of Direct Instructional Procedures

A number of desirable attributes of direct instruction are summarized in Table 7.9. This table is useful not only in evaluating the potential effectiveness of instructional lessons, but also assists the teacher in pinpointing necessary modifications in instructional procedures.

TABLE 7.9

Evaluation of Direct Teacher Instruction

inadequate	adequate	excellent
1	2	3

1	2	3	A. Is an adequate amount of direct teacher instruction provided?
1	2	3	B. Does the teacher use verbal instruction, modelling, and demonstration appropriately?
1	2	3	C. Does the teacher introduce and teach the desired skill/concept directly?
1	2	3	D. Does the instructional lesson provide for gaining and maintaining the learners' attention (e.g., use of visual stimuli, eliciting of child responses, reinforcing of attending and involvement)?
1	2	3	E. Does instruction proceed in small, logical steps?
1	2	3	F. Does the teacher demand intermittent child responses?
1	2	3	G. Is the desired skill or concept described thoroughly prior to eliciting child responses?
1	2	3	H. Do the procedures attempt to reduce potential error responses (e.g., preteach skill before child response, provide clarity of tasks demanded of child, provide a prompt/cue to reduce error responses)?

TABLE 7.8
Application of Correction Procedures

Stimuli Presented to Child	Child's Reponse	Teacher Analysis of Error	Teacher Correction	
"What is the sound of this letter m?"	"The name is m."	Child did not understand the task.	Repeat the task.	"What word."
"Sound out this word." bat	"/d/ /a/ /t/"	Child does not have sufficient information to complete task or was careless.	1. Repeat task to indicate an error to the child.	
			2. Give partial information if not corrected when repeated.	"This sound is /b/. What sound? What word?"
			3. Give entire answer if not corrected when partial information is given.	"This word is bat. What word?"
"Count these objects." O O O O O	"one, two, four, five."	Child does not have sufficient information to complete task or was careless.	1. Repeat task to indicate an error to the child.	"Count these objects. Be careful."
			2. Give entire information. Partial information is not possible on this task.	"Listen to me count: one, two, three, four, five, six. Count with me. Now you count."

113

TABLE 7.9 *Evaluation of Direct Teacher Instruction (cont.)*

1 2 3   I.   Are procedures given for providing feedback on correct responses?

1 2 3   J.   Are procedures given for providing feedback and corrections on errors?

Using the criteria listed in Table 7.9, examine and evaluate this lesson, which introduces the phoneme/grapheme association /ou/ ow, for its potential use with mildly handicapped children.

> Say the following words and have the children listen and tell how they are alike: *cow, now,* and *how.* Have them repeat the words. Write *cow, now,* and *how* on the board in column form and have the children underline the letters in each that are alike. Tell the children that the letters *ow* usually stand for this vowel sound when the sound is heard at the end of a word. Ask them for other words that have this vowel sound at the end. Write their responses on the board and have the letters that stand for the vowel sound identified and underlined. Use Workbook page 15 and Skills Reservoir option: Box B–46 for additional practice. *(The New Macmillan Reading Program,* Level 13.)

Though this lesson might be adequate for many learners, expanding and repeating of instruction on subsequent days would be necessary for the mildy handicapped learner. The lesson did respond to a number of criteria listed: verbal instruction was directly provided on the task, child responses were elicited, information was given before the teacher demanded child responses, and the instruction was broken down into a number of segments. However, the lesson has a number of shortcomings when used with mildly handicapped pupils. The amount of instruction and the number of days on which the skill was taught and reinforced would need expansion. The type of instruction is limited to verbal instruction. (The teacher could also use modeling and demonstration.) Though the lesson elicits child responses, the number of individual and unison responses could be expanded. Most of the elicited responses were not directed at the desired outcome behaviors (before the children are actually required to practice reading words with the target sound). The instruction proceeds in small steps but does not include enough practice at each point. The instruction also ends before the critical behavior (decoding of words) is introduced and practiced. There are no provisions for feedback on correct or error responses. Again, though these shortcomings might not interfere with the typical child in the regular classroom, they might slow the progress of the mildly handicapped child.

INDEPENDENT PRACTICE ACTIVITIES

Although a large amount of classroom time should be spent in direct teacher instruction, a portion of the classroom activities must be exercises that the child can complete independently. The use of independent activities is crucial in order to allow the teacher time to instruct individuals or small groups. In selecting independent practice activities, you must pick those that not only occupy the child but also directly enhance skill development. The major focus of direct teacher instruction is the initial acquisition of new skills. But once the child has gained some proficiency in the desired behavior, he can use the drill and practice of independent practice activities to increase his accuracy and rate of performance.

Extensive modification and expansion of practice activities found in commercial materials are often necessary to accommodate the mildly handicapped learner. Often the practice activities are too few, do not provide adequate practice of new skills, are difficult for the mildly handicapped child to complete, and are too varied in format. Some of these difficulties can be illustrated in the following analysis of one instructional material. We have examined and summarized the practice activities in a math series commonly used in regular education in Table 7.10.

TABLE 7.10
*Analysis of Practice Activities
Provided in a Commercial Material*

Material: Elementary School Mathematics, Book 2

Publisher: Addison Wesley

Year: 1971

Entry Behaviors: 1. One to one correspondence

2. Counting sets to 10

3. Greater than, less than, equal to

4. Writing numerals 0-10

5. Reading number words 0-10

Sequential Steps	*Initial Practice of Skills*		
Place Value	*Number of pages*	*Number of items*	*Number of practice formats*
When given a set of objects, child writes number of 10s to ninety.	1	7	1
When given a set of objects, child writes corresponding 10s and units.	4	38	4
When given sequential numerals to 99, child can write in missing numeral at any point.	4	37	7
When given 2 numbers to 99, child can determine which number is less/more.	5	103	4
When given a set of objects, child can determine number of 10s in one hundred.	1	4	1
When given a set of objects, child writes corresponding 10s and units to 100.	1	4	1
When given sequential numerals to 100, child can write in missing numerals at any point.	2	14	4
When given a numeral, child can write corresponding 100s, 10s, and units.	3	22	2
When given sequential numerals to 999, child can write in missing numerals.	2	10	2

TABLE 7.10 *Analysis of Practice Activities (cont.)*

Math Operation Sequence	Number of pages	Number of items	Number of practice formats
When given two single digits with sums to 10, child can write sum (e.g., $5+2$ =, $4+5$ =).	8	42	6
When given subtraction facts with minuends 1-9, child can write difference. (e.g., $9-3$ = __, $6-2=$ __)	7	34	7
When given mixed addition and subtraction facts, child can write missing numerals in equations to demonstrate INVERSE relationship of addition and subtraction.	5	52	3
When given two addition facts, child can write sum to demonstrate commutative principle.	3	29	3
When given addition facts with sums to 10, child can write missing addends.	4	36	4
When given addition and subtraction facts, child can write missing addends and difference to demonstrate relationships. (e.g. __$+6$ = 10, $10-6$ =__)	2	28	2
When given mixed addition and subtraction facts, child can write sums and differences (e.g., $10-2$ =__, $6+4$ =__)	4	56	4
When given three single-digit addends with sums to 10, child can write sum.	4	28	3

Many difficulties can be pinpointed in this material. First the sequential steps are quite large. For example, all sums to 10 are taught at the same time. The mildly handicapped child would benefit more from many sequential steps leading to all sums to 10. Second, the pace of the material is too fast for a handicapped child. Within the first 30 pages, the child moves from writing numerals to 10 to writing numerals to 999. Third, there is very little actual practice provided at each step. When looking at the number of practice pages, we find that one to seven are provided at each step, yet the total number of practice items is very small. During initial instruction on addition facts to 10, the child is presented with 42 problems, many of which contain prompts on skill performance (e.g., objects to count). The mildly handicapped child and even the normally achieving learner would need far more practice in this skill to reach proficiency. A fourth problem for the handicapped child is the change of formats in the practice activities. Almost every new practice page uses a new practice format. For example, practice on facts to 10 involved six different practice formats (e.g., finding sum with objects present, finding sum involving story problem, finding sum using number line, writing entire equation and finding sum, finding sum using money values). When the practice format continually changes, the child has two pieces of new learning—the *skill* being taught and the *task* used for practice.

When evaluating and modifying practice activities or making your own, ask three questions: (1) Is the practice adequate to lead to skill proficiency? (2) Is the practice relevant to the skill being taught? (3) Can the child perform the practice activities independently?

Amount of Practice Provided

Is the amount of practice adequate for the divergent needs of the mildly handicapped child? Generally the low-performing child will need substantially more practice before mastering a skill. Thus his instructional materials should have many practice activities, which might be provided in workbooks, dittos, or suggested activities found in the teacher's manual. But a mildly handicapped child's movement to a new skill should never be based merely on his completing the practice activities provided in the commercial material. The child's measured performance on the desired skill should be used in determining movement. Practice activities provided in the material should be supplemented with activities from similar materials or those made by the teacher. Other commercial materials are good sources of supplementary practice activities for basic tool subjects (math, spelling, reading, written expression, handwriting).

When you consider the amount of practice provided, examine the number of items; many practice pages demand very few responses. When a page demands only three or four responses from the child, it not only limits the child's practice but also reduces the usefulness of the task as an independent activity. Practice activities are used in the classroom not only to help each child master skills but also to allow the teacher time to instruct other children individually. The independent practice activities must be of adequate length to appropriately occupy the children while the teacher is working with other small groups.

Relevancy of Practice Activities

Appropriate length is only one concern. Practice activities must also be relevant to the needs of the learner. Relevancy is primarily determined by how directly the practice activities are related to an instructional objective deemed important to the individual learner. They must not be "busy work."

You should select practice activities equivalent to the behavior stated in the short-term objective, or analogous activities that alter either the stimulus or the response. If Sally's objective is, "When dictated 20 CVC words with *a,* Sally will be able to write the words with 95% accuracy," you might choose to have her practice this *exact* task or alternate tasks. Equivalent activities would involve your reading the words and Sally's writing the words. Analogous activities would involve a change in stimulus or in the demanded response. For example, Sally could write the words in sentences; look up the words in a dictionary; write a story using the words; or write the words, cover the words, and write them again. As the stimulus and response become more and more distant from the desired behavior, the practice activities lose their potency. To maximize the value of practice, the tasks should be closely matched to the desired outcome behavior. Further examples of equivalent and analogous practice activities are found in table 7.11.

TABLE 7.11

Equivalent and Analogous Independent-Child Interventions

When given a list of fifty CVCe words with vowels *a, i, e, o,* and *u,* Sally will correctly pronounce the words with 95 percent accuracy.

Equivalent practice interventions: Sally reads the words on the list on to a tape which her teacher will listen to later.

Sally reads the list of words to a peer. The peer corrects orally all of Sally's errors.

Analogous practice interventions: Sally reads the words on a language master. The words are printed on the cards. Sally looks at the word, says the word, and then records the word. Sally then listens to the teacher's feedback response recorded on the other audio track.

Sally practices CVCe words on flash cards at her desk. She pronounces the word on the card and then turns the card over to check her response. On the back are short sentences that Sally was dictated that included the focus word. Sally reads these sentences to check if she made a correct response in her initial reading of the word.

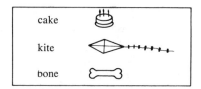

A list of ten words are given to Sally. All of the ten words are objects or action words that can be easily illustrated. Sally writes down the CVCe word, reads the words, and illustrates them.

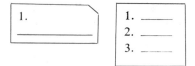

When given an orally read list of twenty-five Dolch words, John will correctly spell all of the twenty-five words.

Equivalent practice interventions: A peer in the classroom reads a word to John. John writes the word. When John completes the list of words, the peer corrects the list of words.

John listens to the words pronounced on language master cards. John writes the word. When John completes the entire list, he corrects his spelling against a key.

TABLE 7.12 *Equivalent and Analogous Independent-Child Interventions (cont.)*

Analogous practice interventions: John is given the list of words with three blank lines after each word. John looks at the first word and copies it in the first blank. Next John covers the word and writes the word by memory in the second blank. After correcting his response, John again covers the word and writes the word by memory in the third blank.

```
the   _____  _____  _____
red   _____  _____  _____
when _____  _____  _____
```

The spelling words are written in large print on a piece of paper. John traces over each of the words five times, pronouncing the word as he traces.

the 〜〜〜

Given the spelling words, John writes each word in one sentence.

   The boy is here.

Independence of Practice Activities

When teaching groups of children, whether in regular or special education, one reality is always present—children must be able to work independently so that the teacher can provide direct teacher instruction to small groups. When evaluating commercial materials, the teacher should consider the potential independence of the activities, always keeping in mind that she can increase the effectiveness of the practice by procedures such as preteaching skills before independent practice, and preteaching tasks before independent completion. The following guidelines are also helpful in increasing the independence of practice activities.

Use simple directions

When directing a child to complete a task, use simple, succinct verbal or written instructions which clearly specify the response demanded of the child. Instructions can often be simplified by altering the vocabulary or by reducing the number of words in the instructions. For example, these directions:

   "On this page you will be working with final punctuation. You are to read each of the sentences and decide what final punctuation mark is the most appropriate. After reading the sentence, write the punctuation at the end of the sentence."

become simpler and more specific when written in this way:

   "Read each sentence. At the end of the sentence add a period, question mark, or exclamation point."

   Directions can be supplemented by examples or demonstration when the task is complex or there are a variety of responses demanded on one assignment.

Use one type of response per page or assignment

If each task demands only one type of response, it is much easier to give simple, consistent instructions. For example, in math a child will have fewer questions when given a worksheet demanding the completion of addition problems than when asked to complete a page that includes addition operations, a few story problems, and an exercise on skip counting. If you want the child to complete a variety of responses, it is helpful to separate them into specific tasks. For example, if you wish the child to complete two sets of responses, place them on separate pages, thus cueing the child that different responses are demanded.

Use standard formats that the child recognizes

Lengthy verbal or written directions are unnecessary if standard formats for independent-practice activities are used. If the child is familiar with the type of response demanded (e.g., *circle* the correct answer), she can respond with maximum independence. This does not mean that you have to limit independent activities to only a few types. Instead, introduce one assignment type and present this format until the child recognizes and responds with total independence. Gradually, the number of tasks that the child understands how to perform can be expanded until the child has learned a large number of response types. If you present two or three novel tasks each day, a great deal of time will be wasted in giving verbal directions, responding to child questions, and guiding the child through her work.

Hold the child accountable for a definite response

The child must always be aware of the exact demands of an assignment and know what she must do to complete the assignment. For example, in these assignments the child knows *exactly* what is expected: "Write each word in a separate sentence"; "Complete page 33"; "Complete the worksheet of 100 subtraction facts"; "Listen to the 25 spelling words on the language master cards and write the words." In the following assignments, the demands are more arbitrary; confusion results when the demands are not implicitly communicated to the child: "Practice your spelling words"; "Read in your basal reader"; "Write sentences using your spelling words." All of these assignments are left to the interpretation of the student. Disruption and disagreement can occur if the interpretation differs from your intent. In these examples, the response demands are not effectively communicated to the child, and she is left to her own interpretation.

Unlike direct teacher instruction, you are not available to give *immediate* feedback on the responses made by the child during independent activities. However, independent child activities allow for a response by the child that can *later* be monitored. This not only increases the value of the task by allowing for feedback, but also increases the accountability of the child. If you direct the child to practice her math fact flash cards at her desk, there is no response that you can examine later and there is no way to ensure that the child has actually performed the desired response. However, you could direct the pupil to: "Practice your flash cards at your desk, and write down the fact and the answer after you have gone through the cards once." In this case, you have accomplished three things: created definite boundaries on the task demanded, added a response that you can examine, and created child accountability by demanding a specific response that you can verify.

Ensure success on the independent child activities

Practice is ineffectual and even damaging when the child practices incorrect responses. You must ensure that the child will not make a large number of errors in her independent practice. For this reason, independent child activities are practices for skills that are beyond the stage of initial acquisition. Verbal and visual prompts used during direct teacher activities can also be used during independent child activities to reduce errors.

Sample Practice Activities

Table 7.12 illustrates an independent practice activity. As you examine it, try to determine its strengths and weaknesses as an independent activity.

TABLE 7.12

Practice activity from New Phonics Skilltext (Charles E. Merrill, 1973)

Working With Words

Circle the base word in each of the words below. Now circle the ending that was added to the base word. In the second row, what letter was doubled before the ending was added?

| scolded | fastest | talking | higher | helped |
| running | biggest | planned | stopping | bobbed |

Say: **golden, beaten, shorten.** What ending does each one have? Add **en** to the words below. Use each new word in the right sentence.

wood_____   eat_____

Squirrels have _____ the nuts. | The fruit was in a _____ dish.

Thinking Back

Say each word below. Listen for the sound of e. Is it long or short? Circle the words in which you hear the long sound of e.

let   eat   she   then   seem   went

Say these words. Listen for the sound of i. Is it long or short? Circle the words in which you hear the short sound of i.

will   mine   him   is   like   cried

Say each word below and listen for the vowel sound of y. Then write the word after the correct heading.

angry   cry   family   shy   sky   shady

y as in by _____   _____   _____

y as in baby _____   _____   _____

Say the name of each picture below. Listen for the ending sound. Then circle the two letters that spell that sound.

th ng wh | sh ch th | ng ch sh | wh sh th

This practice page would be difficult for the handicapped learner for many reasons. It focuses on too many skills on one page; the task continually changes after only a few responses. The directions are very lengthy and demand advanced reading and vocabulary skills. The task demands are not obvious from the page format. The organization of the stimuli leads to confusion and could easily frustrate the learner. Not only is independence hampered in this practice activity, but relevance must also be questioned. Surely the child is not learning all of these skills simultaneously.

Feedback Following the Completion of Independent Practice Activities

Because you are not present when the child is completing independent child activities, special arrangements must be made to allow for feedback on performance during practice sessions. Often teachers collect, correct, and hand papers back. The result is a delay in feedback on performance. Though this feedback is valuable to the child, more immediate feedback would be of additional help. Self-correction of work is one of the best ways of providing this during practice sessions. Correction keys for the assignments—exact duplicates of assignments with answers added—could be available for the child to use following completion of a task. A special correction table, where keys for all assignments given that day are kept, could be a vital part of the classroom organization. A "Correction Pupil" might be chosen each day to monitor the correction table, to assist the child in self-correcting her work, to record data from the assignment, and reduce the number of answers that are altered before the teacher views the work. Problems of cheating are minimized by the use of special procedures: corrections only in red marking pen; no pencils allowed at the correction table; occasional monitoring by you; and presence of a student monitor. Self-correction is maximized if it becomes corrective feedback. The child can provide herself with corrective feedback by redoing or self-correcting her errors. For example, following completion of an addition worksheet, the child could go to the correction table, correct her work by circling errors, examine carefully the correct process on the worksheet, and return to her desk to redo all the problems she missed.

Aides or adult volunteers are often very effective in providing feedback on performance. The adult could be stationed at a desk in the room. As they completed their work, the children could raise their hands. If the adult was free and acknowledged the child, the child could bring her work to the adult for correction. Another alternative is for the adult to rotate among the children working on independent practice activities and provide feedback on problems they were completing. This type of feedback is particularly beneficial because it is immediate and corrective.

Even if self-correction is used in the classroom, you still need to give some verbal feedback after review of the assignments. You might give verbal corrective feedback on three of the eight assignments completed by a child while providing written feedback on the other assignments (e.g., a smiling face on the paper, written comments on how to improve answers, examples added to the page to show a correct procedure, a word rewritten for a misspelled word). In the classroom schedule allow time for verbal corrective feedback on independent practice activities. During a fifteen minute session, you can call individual children to your desk to review certain assignments, or you might return the previous day's work and rotate around the room supplying verbal corrective feedback to reinforce the written feedback given on the paper: "Sally, let's look at your spelling words. You are missing the words

baking, talking, and *riding.* Remember to drop the *e,* before you add the *ing.*'';
"Tom, on your math paper I circled the nine problems that you missed. In all of
these problems you were not careful in making the numbers *one* and *seven.*''; "Rob,
your creative writing was really great yesterday. You wrote more words and
remembered all of the capitals and periods."

When the child is at the proficiency stage, communication of feedback should
not only include corrective feedback, but should communicate the child's progress
toward her goal. This includes communicating her present performance in
relationship to past performance, and present performance in relationship to a goal.
A child should know the level of performance you are demanding before she moves
to a new skill. This communication of progress will often add needed motivation to
skill performance. The use of self-charting or graphing is often a very effective
technique at this point. The child can keep a daily record of her performance on a
given task. By charting her performance, the child will receive immediate feedback
on how she is progressing toward her goal.

Modification of Practice Activities

If practice activities prove to be inadequate, the teacher may wish to make minor
modifications which would allow students to complete the exercises successfully and
independently. Table 7.13 outlines some of these potential modifications.

TABLE 7.13

Modifications in practice activities

Problem	Possible Modifications
Does not include enough items	Pair with other similar tasks.
Does not have enough practice activities	Supplement with teacher-made activities. Supplement with activities from other commercial materials.
Directions are too difficult	Verbally present the tasks. Pair the worksheet with an auditory tape that explains directions. Add examples to the practice page. Go through a number of items during small group instruction. Write alternate sets of directions. Highlight the important words in the directions (underline, use marking pen). Pair children with better readers to assist them when directions are difficult.
Too many tasks are presented on the page	Cut the page into a number of segments. Visually cue the change of task on the page (e.g., draw a line between tasks).
No feedback and correction procedures are provided	Make correction keys for practice activities. Set aside time to review pages with children. Designate peer as "paper checker." Correct as a group during direct teacher instruction.

Summary

Independent practice activities have two purposes in the classroom: to provide relevant practice on a skill or concept and to provide independent activities for children to complete when the teacher is providing instruction to classmates. To achieve the first goal, the practice activities, whether selected from a commercial or teacher-made material, must relate directly to an instructional objective for the child, must not be busy work, and must be preceded by direct teacher instruction. By carefully phrasing the directions, controlling the number of different responses demanded by the activity and the general appearance of the task, and preteaching the necessary entry behaviors, the teacher can better ensure that children will be able to complete the activities independently. As we have noted, the potential for in-dependent completion of the activities, their relevancy to the child's instructional program, and the amount of practice provided must be considered. The low-per-forming or mildly handicapped child will need more practice than the normally progressing child, thus demanding commercial materials with many opportunities for practice or supplementation with other materials. Since most practice activities used come from commercially published materials, selection of appropriate material is essential. The questions in table 7.14 will assist you in selecting practice activities as well as in evaluating activities you develop.

TABLE 7.14

Evaluation Of Practice Activities

1 2 3   A. Does the material contain an adequate amount of practice?

           yes no   1. Does the material include an adequate number of practice activities?

           yes no   2. Does the material include supplementary practice ac-tivities?

           yes no   3. Do the practice activities have enough items to occupy the child and provide enough practice?

1 2 3   B. Is the practice relevant?

           yes no   1. Does the practice relate directly to a behavioral ob-jective?

           yes no   2. Does the practice follow up direct teacher instruction?

           yes no   3. Do the practice activities avoid busy work?

           yes no   4. Are the practice tasks closely related to the desired out-come behavior (close match of stimulus and response)?

1 2 3   C. Can the practice activities be completed independently?

           yes no   1. Are the skills demanded in practice activities pretaught?

           yes no   2. Are tasks demanded in practice activities pretaught?

           yes no   3. Does the material use a limited number of tasks and avoid the continuous use of novelty?

           yes no   4. Does the material use simple practice formats?

           yes no   5. Are the response demands obvious from the format?

TABLE 7.14 *Evaluation of Practice Activities (cont.)*

yes no	6.	Are simple directions (verbal or written) provided?
yes no	7.	Are the directions paired with examples of task performance?
yes no	8.	Are the supportive skills on practice pages easier than the skill being taught?

1 2 3   D. Are feedback procedures provided in the material?

inadequate	adequate	excellent
1	2	3

SUMMARY OF THE SELECTION OF MATERIALS

In selecting materials, you have three options: (1) to *adopt* commercial material; (2) to *adapt* commercial material to the specific instructional needs of the child; and (3) to *make* materials. To make instruction of the mildly handicapped feasible within the regular class, commercially prepared materials should be used when possible. This practice not only reduces preparation time but also allows the teacher to use the expertise of authors and publishers. If carefully selected, and modified when necessary, regular classroom materials can be used successfully with the mildly handicapped child.

The major criteria to be used in selecting instructional material for potential use with the mildly handicapped or low-performing child have been discussed throughout the preceding chapters, and are summarized in table 7.15.

TABLE 7.15

Evaluation and Selection of Materials

Instruction

1. Are instruction procedures for each lesson clearly specified?

2. Does the material provide a maximum amount of direct teacher instruction on the skills/concepts presented?

3. Does the direct teacher instruction provide for active student involvement and responses?

4. Are the direct instructional lessons adaptable to small-group/individual instruction?

5. Is a variety of cueing and prompting techniques used to elicit correct child responses?

6. When using verbal instruction, does the instruction proceed in a clear, logical fashion?

7. Does the teacher use modeling and demonstration when appropriate to the skills being taught?

8. Does the material specify correction and feedback procedures for use during instruction?

Practice

1. Does the material contain appropriate practice activities that contribute to mastery of the skills/concepts?

2. Are the practice activities directly related to the desired outcome behaviors?

TABLE 7.15 *Evaluation and Selection of Materials (cont.)*

3. Does the material provide enough practice for the slow learner?

4. Does the material provide for feedback on responses during practice?

5. Can the learner complete practice activities independently?

6. Does the material reduce the probability of error in independent practice activities?

Sequence of Instruction

1. Are the scope and sequence of the material clearly specified?

2. Are facts/concepts/skills ordered in a logical manner from simple to complex?

3. Does the sequence proceed in small steps, easily attainable by the handicapped learner?

Content

1. Does the selection of the concepts and skills adequately represent the content area?

2. Is the content consistent with the stated objectives?

3. Is the information presented in the material accurate?

4. Is the information presented in the material current?

5. Are various points of view concerning treatment of minorities and handicapped people, ideologies, social values, sex roles, socioeconomic class, etc., objectively represented?

6. Are the content and topic of the material relevant to the needs of the handicapped students as well as to the other students in the regular classroom?

Behavioral Objectives

1. Are objectives clearly stated for the material?

2. Are the objectives consistent with the goals for the whole classroom?

3. Are the objectives stated in behavioral terms including the desired child behavior, the criteria for measurement of the behavior, and the desired standard of performance?

Entry Behaviors

1. Does the material specify the prerequisite student skills needed to work with ease in the material?

2. Are the prerequisite student skills compatible with the objectives of the material?

Initial Assessment/placement

1. Does the material provide a method to determine initial placement into the material?

2. Does the initial placement tool contain enough items to accurately place the learner into the material?

Ongoing Assessment/evaluation

1. Does the material provide evaluation procedures for measuring progress and mastery of objectives?

2. Are there sufficient evaluative items to accurately measure learner progress?

3. Are procedures and/or materials for ongoing record keeping provided?

TABLE 7.15 *Evaluation and Selection of Materials (cont.)*

Review/maintenance

1. Are practice and review of content material provided?

2. Are review and maintenance activities systematically and appropriately spaced?

3. Are adequate review and maintenance activities provided for the slow learner?

Motivation/interest

1. Are reinforcement procedures built in or suggested for use in the program?

2. Are procedures specified for providing feedback to the student on his/her progress?

3. Has the program been designed to motivate and appeal to students?

Adaptability to Individual Differences

1. Can the pace be adapted to variations in learner rate of mastery?

2. Can the method of response be adapted to the individual needs of the learner?

3. Can the method of instruction be adapted to the individual needs of the learner?

4. Can the child advance to subsequent tasks when he has demonstrated proficiency?

5. Can the learner be placed in the material at his own level?

6. Does the material offer alternative teaching strategies for students who are failing to master an objective?

Physical Characteristics of the Material

1. Is the format uncluttered?

2. Is the format grammatically correct and free of typographical errors?

3. Are photographs and illustrations clear, attractive, and consistent with the content?

4. Are the type size and style appropriate to the students?

5. Are auditory components of adequate clarity and amplification?

6. Are the materials durable?

7. Can the materials be easily stored and organized for classroom use?

Teacher Considerations

1. Is a teacher's manual or set of teacher guidelines provided?

2. Are teacher instructions clear, complete, and unambiguous?

3. Does the material specify the skills and abilities needed by the instructor to work effectively with the material?

8

MONITORING THE INSTRUCTIONAL PROGRAM

ONGOING ASSESSMENT OF PERFORMANCE

Assessment is a process that must continue throughout the school year if you are to determine when a child has mastered an objective or when the child's progress is slow and you need to modify your instruction. Precise and systematic teaching depends on a teacher who is constantly aware of the child's performance so that decisions can be made to efficiently use instructional time.

Benefits of Ongoing Assessment

Ongoing assessment of student performance consumes both the time and energy of the teacher and his students. Most teachers use these procedures only with specific children who are experiencing difficulty in learning, and then only in the specific skill areas in which those children are experiencing the most difficulty. To ignore these procedures is to have numbers of children continue to fail in our schools.

Teacher benefits

The benefits of ongoing assessment are especially apparent in program planning. A data recording system provides information which you can use to decide when a child has mastered an objective and is ready to move to a new objective. Records remove much of the arbitrariness that often occurs in program planning, either by retaining a child too long in a particular program or by moving the child on before he has truly mastered the skill. From the information collected you can also assess the adequacy of the child's performance. If you are not satisfied with his progress,

---

Anita Archer

you may alter your instructional activities, "slice back" the skill, or program a new or lower level task.

Your personal benefits should not be minimized. The mildly handicapped child may have slower rates of growth; his change might not be as apparent as that of other children in the classroom. The data collected illustrates the efforts of the child. Such data will often be your payoff, a reward for your individual efforts with a child. It is very exciting to see that the child can change and benefit from an instructional program.

Child benefits

The child will receive a better program when decisions are based on data and not made arbitrarily. It is often easier to move a child to a new skill when the workbook is filled up, or to maintain him on a step too long because the next step has not been prepared, than to base the decisions on the more important information concerning the child's *actual* performance. When you base decisions on data collection, you are more likely to continually evaluate the effectiveness of the program and change the program when it does not produce change. Likewise, you will move the child to a new skill when mastery has occurred.

Communication benefits

If the data are to be useful to you, the child, parents, and other support personnel, you must select a method for ongoing assessment that clearly reflects the child's progress toward meeting his long-range instructional objectives in language that is concrete, concise, and free of unnecessary jargon.

By using data, you can let the child know how close he is to achieving his goals. Other professionals working with the child, such as the school's speech therapist, psychologist, social worker, or resource room teacher can also use your data to make informed team decisions on the child's needs.

Clarity in data recording is particularly important when you communicate with the child's parents. Objective data on the specific skills being taught will often reduce the emotional factor in discussions concerning the handicapped child. Also, such data focus on what the child is actually doing and on what skills he is learning, instead of on the differences between the child and others in the classroom. Parents are gratified by the professionalism and accountability of the teacher as reflected in data recording.

Ongoing assessment plays a particularly critical role in serving children for whom an IEP has been established. The child's progress toward the long-term goals and mastery of the short-term objectives must be measured and evaluated at least annually. Ideally the teacher should collect periodic or daily data on the child's performance when teaching specific objectives. These data can be recorded and summarized and used to evaluate the child's growth in the educational program prescribed in the IEP.

Deciding What to Measure

It is not necessary to measure and assess every behavior that occurs in the classroom. A method of assessment should be developed, however, for the areas chosen as the prime focus for the mildly handicapped child. These areas of focus were determined from the initial assessment data and were stated in the form of short-term objectives which guide the formulation of the data recording procedures. For example, if the objective states that Sally will read words "when given a list of fifty CVC words with a short *a*," the behavior will be measured under these *conditions*. The *standard*, or criterion, set in the objective determines the aspects of the behavior to be measured (e.g., if the standard includes a percentage of accuracy, you will measure correct and incorrect responses occurring during the task and compute a percentage score; if the standard sets a desired rate on a certain task, the number of behaviors occurring in a time period will be counted). Thus, the short-term objective helps determine an assessment procedure for each skill.

Measuring all occurrences of the behavior

When measuring nonacademic behaviors that have a low frequency, you may wish to count all occurrences during the day. Incidents of swearing, following directions, raising hand for teacher's help, or walking around the room could be noted by the teacher throughout the day, and a total frequency for the behavior determined. As with all data collected, this would allow comparison with performance on previous and subsequent days and monitoring of the effectiveness of the behavioral interventions (programming for nonacademic behaviors will be discussed in chapter 9).

Probing of a behavior or time sampling

In academic behaviors, we seldom measure all occurrences of the behavior; rather, we sample the academic behavior. For example, Sally is given four exercises during math period to practice her addition facts: by flash cards, a tachistoscope, Language Master, and worksheet. For assessment purposes, only performance on the flash cards might be used. You will certainly evaluate the other responses in order to give Sally feedback, but only the number of correct and incorrect responses on the twenty flash cards are carefully examined and recorded. Sampling behavior is often referred to as a *probe*. Examples of probes include: following completion of two practice pages, a one-minute probe is taken on division facts; after a story in a basal reader is completed, a one-minute probe is taken on oral paragraph reading; and at the beginning of an instructional group, a two-minute probe of writing cursive letters is taken, followed by four more practice worksheets in which the teacher gives feedback on the formation of each letter.

When monitoring nonacademic behavioral programs, you may also elect to sample the behavior rather than count all occurrences of the behavior. In this case, you take a time-sampling of the behavior, a count of the behavior during a limited period of time in the classroom. When the nonacademic behavior occurs at such a high frequency that you would be spending a great deal of time recording and counting the occurrences of the behavior, choose to measure the behavior during a specific activity or time segment (e.g., John may swear throughout the day; however, you decide to count swearing only during art period) and use these data to evaluate the effectiveness of the intervention which could be in effect throughout the entire day.

Deciding on the Dimensions of the Behavior to Measure

Many aspects of behavior can be measured, but only the most appropriate dimensions of the behavior must be selected to match the objective. For the objective of reading words from a sight vocabulary list, the number of words that a child reads could be counted. Instead of counting the number of words, the number of correct and incorrect words could be counted. Or, by adding a time factor, a rate of correct and incorrect responses could be recorded. A number of techniques can be used, depending on how the teacher plans to use the data.

Occurence and non-occurrence of a behavior

Occasionally you will want to know simply whether a behavior does or does not occur. For example, you want to know: Can the child read specific words such as *there, what,* and *want* on sight vocabulary lists of irregular words? Can the child write the numerals 1, 2, 3, 4, or 5? Can he name the colors blue, red, yellow, white, or black? When we are interested in whether or not a specific behavior or group of behaviors occurs, we ask the child to perform each task once and record whether he can or cannot perform the behavior.

Accuracy

In teaching basic subjects, particularly at the stage of initial acquisition, our primary concern is accuracy. When collecting accuracy data, record correct and incorrect responses on a specific task and compute a percentage score that allows comparison of performance across days.

Rate

If speed as well as accuracy is critical to successful performance of the skill, you may wish to add a time factor to your data. For example, it is important that children read words not only accurately but fluently, that they compute mathematical facts not only accurately but quickly. For these skills, simply record the number of correct and incorrect responses on a minute sample of the task. Rate can also be used for nonacademic behaviors such as the number of times a child is out of his seat during an hour's math class, or the number of times in an hour that a child talks out. Again, rate measures add precision to the simple count of child behaviors and allow you to compare the child's performance on a number of days.

Duration

For some behaviors, you will be concerned with the duration of the behavior rather than rate. In these cases you measure the length of time engaged in a behavior. You may want to know how long a young child spends playing with peers or the amount of time spent working at his desk completing work. The teacher of the older child may wish to measure the length of time the child spends reading recreational materials, the amount of time spent coming in from recess, or the amount of time spent talking with friends during work time.

In any event, the type of data you collect will depend on the objective and how you plan to use the data. In all cases, the data need to be used to make instructional decisions.

Deciding How Often to Measure

You must decide exactly how often the behavior will be measured. Behaviors may be measured daily or at least often enough to be used in decision making. Daily data will give you continuous information on which to base changes in interventions, programs, or objectives. However, certain behaviors may be measured less frequently (e.g., Mondays and Wednesdays); this method is especially useful for behaviors where change occurs less frequently, for data that is kept on a review basis, or for time-consuming measurement techniques.

Pre- and posttests

Pre- and posttests have long been used in the regular classroom. When using pre- and posttests, the same or similar tests are administered to the child. The pretest indicates if instruction is needed on a particular skill and the posttest verifies if the skill has been mastered. Though pre- and posttests are effective in communicating growth on a desired behavior, they are less effective in assisting the teacher in decision making. Though posttests answer the question, "Has the child mastered the skill?" they do not answer the formative questions, "Is the child improving as a result of instruction?" or "Is different instruction needed to alter the child's performance?"

Daily data

To better assist the teacher in program planning and modification, data should be collected more frequently than at the beginning and end of instruction on a specific skill. If the child is receiving daily instruction and practice on a skill, daily measurement is recommended. When daily data are collected, you have a continuous record of child performance, you know exactly when the child has met the criterion in your objective, and you have information that could justify a change in instruction or practice procedures. Daily data are particularly important when rapid skill acquisition is expected due to small-step instruction. For example, you might test the child daily on writing his new cursive letters, on oral reading in his basal reader, or on such nonacademic behaviors as remaining in his seat or talking out in class.

Less frequent data

For some behaviors, particularly when the measurement takes a good deal of time or when many children are in need of special help, you may prefer to measure the behavior periodically, such as once a week or every third day. You might choose to give a spelling list every third day instead of every day or to give a vocabulary review test on Tuesday and Thursday. Though this technique of periodic sampling does not supply you with the precise feedback on your programming given by daily measurement, it is certainly more helpful in program monitoring than pre- and posttest measures only. The use of periodic data is particularly appropriate when rapid change in skill development would not be expected, and for review testing.

Consistent Events

In a short-term objective, the conditions under which the desired behavior will occur are stated. These conditions will be used to establish a consistent measurement that can be used over time. For example, if the short-term objective states that John will name the numbers when presented with numerals 1 to 10 on flash cards, then a consistent event will be established where John will be asked to name the numerals presented on the flash cards. You should attempt to control as many aspects of the measurement event as possible. Varying the presentation method, the time of day, the person taking the data, the type of stimulus given, and the type of response expected can alter the data collected. When these factors are altered, the data collected daily cannot be directly compared. When the measurement event is not held constant, the data may not reflect true growth in the skill. For example, one might expect some change in response on these two days.

MONDAY: The teacher gave Sue thirty flash cards of addition facts with sums to ten. Sue orally gave the answers to the problems and the teacher recorded the number of correct answers to the flash cards.

TUESDAY: The teacher gave Sue a worksheet containing thirty addition facts with sums to ten. Sue returned to her seat where she completed the problems by writing down the answers. The teacher then corrected the worksheet and noted the number of correct answers to the addition facts.

In order to maintain comparability of data collected, you need to use a constant data event over time. However, you should exercise caution when keeping items on probes exactly the same day after day. The child may memorize the first five words on a sight vocabulary probe or the first ten answers on a multiplication fact probe and thus not be proficient in a skill, even though he does well on the probe. Though you should control the exact type of items presented on a probe, randomizing their presentation will prevent simple memorization.

Deciding How to Record the Data

A method of recording should be selected that is easy to maintain, that is appropriate to the type of data collected and the skill measured, and that effectively communicates to those using the data.

Raw data

For some of the behaviors measured in the classroom, only the raw data may be recorded. For example, you may keep a simple record each day of the number of occurrences of a behavior. This tabulation of frequency of occurrence might be kept for such behaviors as inappropriately talking out in class, swearing, hitting other children, or leaving the classroom without permission. A simple tally sheet such as illustrated in Table 8.1 might be appropriate for counting behaviors by frequency of occurrence.

Raw data might also record the number of correct and incorrect responses for a specific behavior. To make data easily comparable over time, control the possible number of trials during which the child can perform. For example, you might give the child twenty-five sight words to read each day. You could keep the number of words constant, and then record the number of correct and incorect responses. A possible format for recording this raw data is illustrated in Tables 8.2 and 8.3.

A checklist is another device that can be used in recording raw data. This record indicates if the child can or cannot perform a specific task. Usually the child is given only one trial and the teacher records if the child correctly or incorrectly performed the skill. This recording device effectively indicates sight words read, colors named, numerals named, words spelled correctly, components of a self-help task completed, or addition problems correctly answered. This type of recording device is used in Table 8.4 to record sight words read on consecutive days.

TABLE 8.1

Tally Sheet Used to Record Raw Data

Tally Sheet:	Date	Talk-outs
Number of talk-outs are tabulated on daily tally sheets	4/5	/////////
	4/6	/////////
	4/7	///////////
	4/8	///////
	4/11	//////////
	4/12	/////
	4/13	//

NOTE: In this example the teacher is counting the number of talk-outs (speaking when inappropriate according to class rules) by a child during the day. The teacher kept a simple tally sheet at his desk. When he heard the child make an inappropriate talk-out he added a tally mark. The teacher kept this data each day. On April 13, the teacher initiated a program in which the child received free time (positive reinforcement) for no talk-outs in an hour's period of time.

TABLE 8.2

Recording Correct and Incorrect Responses on Spelling Tests

Name   *Arlene*

Date	Spelling List #	C/E (possible 12)	
4/6	#1	C 7	E 5
4/7	#1	C 9	E 3
4/8	#1	C 12	E 0
4/11	#2	C 4	E 8
4/12	#2	C 5	E 7
4/13	#2	C 12	E 0
4/14	#3	C 7	E 5
4/15	#3	C 9	E 3

TABLE 8.2 *Recording Correct and Incorrect Responses on Spelling Tests (cont.)*

4/18	#3	C *11*	E *1*
4/19	#4	C *3*	E *9*

C = Correct response   E = Error response

NOTE: The teacher established this data recording sheet for his spelling program. Word lists for spelling were prewritten, twelve words appearing on each list. The word lists were numbered so that the teacher could easily indicate the focus list on the data recording sheet. After the spelling test was taken each day, the teacher recorded the number of correct and incorrect responses on the data sheet. When the child received a score of at least eleven words correct, a new list was presented.

TABLE 8.3

Recording Correct and Incorrect Responses on Different Tasks

Name   *John Scott*

Date

Objective	Interventions										
When given 25 flash cards with sums to 10, John will correctly solve all the problems.	Language master practice; daily drill by volunteer; completion of two worksheets.	C	C	C	C	C	C	C	C	C	C
		E	E	E	E	E	E	E	E	E	E
When given 20 oral numbers to 100, John will correctly write the numeral.	Language master; peer practice on writing numerals.	C	C	C	C	C	C	C	C	C	C
		E	E	E	E	E	E	E	E	E	E
When given a clock set at 20 different times to the hour, John will correctly tell time.	Practice work-sheets on writing time; time telling game with peer.	C	C	C	C	C	C	C	C	C	C
		E	E	E	E	E	E	E	E	E	E

C = Correct response   E = Error response

NOTE: This data recording device was designed to record progress on three objectives for John in math. In the first box, the objective is written out indicating the consistent measurement event to be used and the criterion for movement to a new skill. In the second box, independent-child activities are listed. Each day following the measurement activity the teacher records number of correct responses and number of errors on the task.

Computed data

To make the raw data easier to compare across time and to increase the effectiveness of communication, you may wish to compute the data. Computed scores may involve the calculation of percentages of correct and incorrect responses, and the rate of their occurrence within a specified time period. For example, you might note that when given twenty-five sentences, Sally correctly used final punctuation in twenty of

TABLE 8.4

Example of Checklist Used for Recording Known Sight Words

Name   *Tom*   CORRECT +   ERROR 0

WORD ABLE	M	T	W	T	F	M	T	W	T (Review)	F	M	T	W	T (Review)	F
about	0	0	+	+	+				+					+	
above	0	0	+	+	+				+					+	
across	0	+	+	0	+	+	+		+					+	
after	0	+	+	+					+					+	
again	0	0	0	+	+	+			+					+	
almost	0	0	0	+	+	+			+					+	
alone	0	+	+	+					0	0	+	+	+	+	
already	0	0	0	+	0	+	+	+	+					0	+
always	0	0	0	+	0	+	+	+	0					+	
another	0	0	+	+	+				+					+	
any						0	+	0	+	+	+			+	
art						0	0	0	+	0	+	+	+	+	
because						0	+	0	0	+	+	+		+	
been						0	+	+	+					+	
before						0	0	0	+	+	+			+	
behind						0	+	+	+					+	
believe						0	0	0	0	0	0	+	+	+	
batter								0	0	+	+	+		+	
between										0	+	+	+	+	
board										0	+	0	0	+	+
both											+	+	+	+	
brought												0	0	0	0
all													+	+	+
called													0	0	+
came													0	+	0
car															0
change															0
church															0

NOTE: This checklist was devised to record the responses made by Tom on sight words each day. At the beginning of an instructional period, the teacher presents ten words to Tom on flash cards. The teacher records a circle for an incorrect response and a plus for a correct response. If Tom says a word correctly for three consecutive days, the mastered word is dropped from his word list and a new word is added. Each Thursday the teacher gives a review list of all words previously mastered. If Tom makes an error on a previously mastered list, the word that is incorrect will be added again to the study list.

twenty-five trials, or on 80 percent of the items. When given twenty division facts, John made two errors, for a score of 90 percent. You may be interested in determining a rate for a specified task. For example, when given a paragraph of 100 words, Fred completed the paragraph in two minutes; his oral reading rate was 50 words per minute. (See Table 8.5 for an example of recording percentage scores).

Data recording devices can often be effectively combined with planning sheets designed to record objectives, interventions, and the daily data collected on the child's performance. Record on the sheet the number of possible items on the measurement task, the number of correct and incorrect responses, and then compute the percentage. When the child masters an objective, a line is drawn to indicate mastery (see Table 8.6).

TABLE 8.5

Example of Data Recording Device Using Percentage Scores

Name *Mary S.*   Skill area *Multiplication*

Step on Sequence	Date begun	Percentage Score								Date Mastered	Review Scores
1 dig × 2 dig cue	1/3	22%	67%	79%	95%					1/7	
1 dig × 2 dig	1/10	25%	38%	46%	36%	54%	83%	87%	91%		
		94%	96%							1/21	
1 dig × 3 dig	1/24	84%	86%	90%	95%					1/28	
1 dig × 4 dig	1/31	76%	84%	90%	98%					2/4	
2 dig × 2 d'g cue	2/7	52%	39%	81%	72%	63%	85%	87%	89%	2/18	
		91%	95%								
2 dig × 2 dig	2/21	77%	81%	93%	95%					2/24	
2 dig × 3 dig cue	2/25	68%	73%	91%	90%	97%					
2 dig × 3 dig	3/2										

NOTE: Percentage scores are recorded on this recording device. In the left column, the teacher writes the sequential step or short-term objective, followed by the date the child began practice on the skill. On each consecutive day, a percentage score is recorded until the child meets the desired criterion (95 percent in this example). When the child meets the desired criterion, the date of mastery is noted and a new skill written in. The review column is used to record scores on periodic maintenance assignments. The lower level multiplication skills are maintained by practice on the more difficult tasks. For this reason no specific review exercises were given. However, this column would be very important in the maintenance of skills not practiced through other exercises in the classroom.

Graphs

The use of graphs is often the most effective way to display data. The graph illustrates visually the changes in performance on specific objectives. Graphs can be used to aid teachers in making instructional decisions and to communicate ef-

TABLE 8.6

Plan Sheet and Data Recording Sheet Combined

Name _____

OBJECTIVE	MONDAY	TUESDAY	WEDNESDAY	THURSDAY	FRIDAY
	◯	◯	◯	◯	◯
	P C E %	P C E %	P C E %	P C E %	P C E %
C.M.					
	◯	◯	◯	◯	◯
	%	%	%	%	%
C.M.					
	◯	◯	◯	◯	◯
	%	%	%	%	%
C.M.					
	◯	◯	◯	◯	◯
	%	%	%	%	%
C.M.					
	◯	◯	◯	◯	◯
	P C E %	P C E %	P C E %	P C E %	P C E %
C.M.					

C.M. = criterion for movement to a new skill   E = error responses
  P   = possible number of items   ◯ = number of days on objective
  C   = correct responses

NOTE: On this recording sheet, both raw data and the converted percentage scores are listed. This device can be used to record all objectives in one subject area for a child or objectives in different skill areas. On the left the objective is written in. The abbreviation *C.M.* stands for the criterion or standard that the child must reach before moving to a new skill. In the individual boxes, the teacher will write the interventions used for the objective on that day.

fectively to the child, other professionals, and to parents. Children too are very interested in graphs of their behaviors; sometimes these graphs serve as positive reinforcers to the student. Graphs are particularly useful because of their flexibility and the number of dimensions that can be recorded (see Figures 8.1 and 8.2). Possible dimensions that could be recorded include:

1. date

2. number of correct or incorrect responses

3. the frequency of a behavior

4. the number of such responses per specified time period

5. the percentage of accuracy of the behavior

6. the amount of time in which a behavior occurred

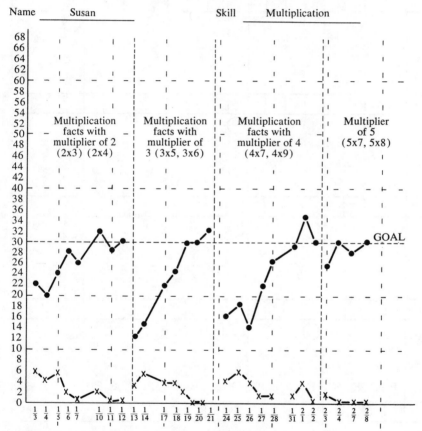

Number of correct responses (●) and incorrect responses (x) on one-minute probe.

NOTE: Though the teacher provided Susan with many interventions on multiplication facts, he used a one-minute probe for the consistent measurement event. Each day Susan was given a one-minute probe on multiplication facts. The teacher corrected the page with Susan. Susan then plotted the number of correct responses and the number of incorrect responses on this graph. (The criterion of movement was ● 30 correct responses in a minute, and no errors.)

FIGURE 8.1. *Graphic Display of Correct and Incorrect Responses in One-minute Probe on Multiplication Facts*

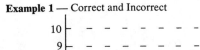

Example 1 — Correct and Incorrect

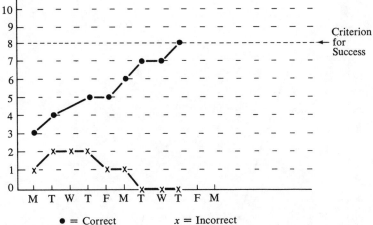

● = Correct   x = Incorrect

NOTE: Number of correct and incorrect responses to
reading comprehension questions. Eight questions per
day. Criterion for success was eight right, no errors.

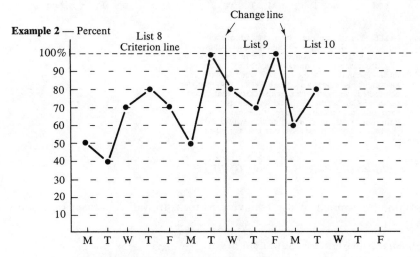

NOTE: Percentage of correct spelling words on daily
probe of ten words. 100 per cent correct for movement
was criterion for new list.

FIGURE 8.2 *Examples of Graphic Display*

Summary

A well-written instructional objective is prerequisite to the data recording system. This objective guides the choice of the behavior to be measured, the conditions under which it will be measured, and the standard of performance for success. After writing a short-term objective, you will:

1. determine the dimension of the behavior to be measured (for example, frequency, rate, correct and error responses, or duration);

2. determine how often to measure the behavior (daily or less frequently);

Example 3 — Duration

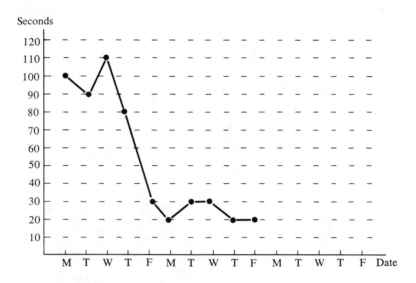

Seconds

NOTE: Length of time from verbal question by teacher until Gary begins verbal reply. Two questions per day. Gary was of concern to the teacher because he did not respond to questions asked by the teacher during group discussion time, even when he knew the answer. This chart was begun after the teacher contracted an agreement with Gary that every response Gary made during discussion time would earn him one minute of free time before recess. Criterion for success (for the teacher) was less than a total duration of twenty seconds in a period of two days.

FIGURE 8.2 *Examples of Graphic Display (cont.)*

3. determine how much of the behavior to measure (all responses or a sampling); and

4. establish a consistent measurement event.

You then record the data (e.g., by tally sheet, checklist, computed score, or graph) to facilitate decision making and communication with others. (An example of these procedures is given in Table 8.7.)

TABLE 8.7

Planning a Data Recording System

Steps in Establishing a System	Example
Step 1: Write a measurable short-term objective.	During the one-hour math period, Charlie will not get out of his seat except to come to group instruction.

TABLE 8.7 *Planning a Data Recording System (cont.)*

Step 2: Determine the dimensions of the behavior that you wish to measure.	I wish to measure the number of times Charlie gets out of his seat during the one-hour math period. The important dimension that I will focus on will be frequency of occurrence during the one-hour time period.
Step 3: Decide how often you wish to measure the behavior.	I will measure this behavior each day during math period.
Step 4: Decide how much of the behavior you wish to measure and record.	I will record all occurrences of the behavior during the math period.
Step 5: Establish a consistent measurement event.	Math period will always include seat work on operations, facts and story problems. During math period, Charlie will come to the math table for ten minutes of direct teacher instruction.
Step 6: Decide how to record the data.	During math period, I will keep a tally sheet on my desk and mark any time Charlie is out of his seat except when he is given permission. At the end of the math period, I will add up the tally marks and record the number of times he was out of his seat.

Date	Number of times out of seat	
3/8	//////	6
3/9	//////	6
3/10	///	3
3/11	//	2
3/12	/	1
3/15	/	1

PROGRAM MODIFICATIONS

Modifications in a specific child's program should be based on the child's performance data. The data from the ongoing assessment procedures enable the teacher to answer two specific questions: Has the child mastered the skill sufficiently to move on to a new skill objective? Is the child making satisfactory progress in the current program? When teachers use well-formulated short-term objectives with specific criteria for mastery, the first question (mastery) is easy to answer. As soon as the child has demonstrated the skill level stated in the objective, you need to begin instruction on the next skill in the sequence (see Figure 8.3). The answer to the second question (When is progress satisfactory?) is somewhat more difficult. When you determine that progress is not satisfactory, changes must be made in the instructional program.

Indicators of Unsatisfactory Progress

Comparison to previous rate of acquisition

By consistently monitoring performance data, you are always aware of student progress on a specific objective. Although many factors influence how quickly a child will reach mastery criterion, by comparing the child's previous rate of mastery in a related skill area you may discover a child who is not progressing as expected. For example, if a child reached mastery criterion on the five tables in multiplication in six days, but after sixteen days on the six tables was still experiencing difficulties, you would want to consider changing the instructional program. On the other hand, a child who learned one list of ten spelling words to criterion level in four days, could still be considered to be progressing satisfactorily after five days on another list. You need to use previous acquisition rates as *one* guideline in determining if the child's progress is satisfactory.

Another example of using previous acquisition rates pertains to skills which you might expect the child to learn more rapidly and with greater ease because of their similarity to earlier mastered skills. For example, a child is expected to learn one-digit times three-digit multiplication faster than she learned one-digit times two-digit multiplication because she has already mastered the major components of the more complex skill. Thus, if a child mastered one-digit times two-digit multiplication in ten days and had not mastered one-digit times three-digit multiplication by the twelfth day of instruction, you should consider modification of the instructional program.

No change in performance

One of the most noticeable data trends is no change in child performance over a period of time. This data pattern should be a red flag that some change is needed in the instructional program. For example, a teacher has selected for one student a short-term objective of fifty correct words a minute in oral reading. After six consecutive days at twenty correct words a minute, a modification in the instructional program would be an appropriate decision. Even more obvious is the child who on five consecutive days has 100 percent errors on his two-place, regroup subtraction problems. A simple rule of thumb is that no progress on the child's part indicates needed change in instructional programming.

Feedback from children

Children are the source of one type of information that is available nowhere else: how they feel about their own progress. Teachers who attend to this information are capable of vastly improving their timing when making modifications in a child's instructional program. You need to be aware of two types of child behavior which may indicate the need for program modification: direct verbal comments from the child, and nonverbal, off-task behaviors. When asked, children will often tell you exactly what is confusing about a particular instructional procedure; you should act

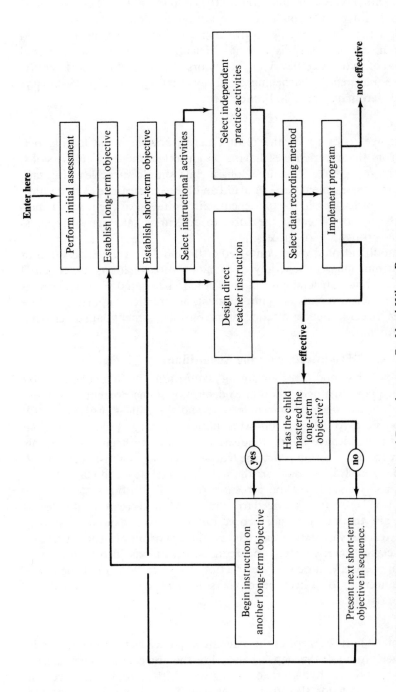

FIGURE 8.3. *Systematic Instructional Procedures to Be Used When Program Is Effective*

on this information quickly. Simple questions to the child might be, "Do you understand what you are to do?" "Do you have any questions?" You may also save a lot of program revision time by attending to the many nonverbal or tangential child behaviors that indicate the child is having difficulties with the instructional program. Any type of avoidance behavior (behaviors that keep the child from the task) such as continual pencil sharpening or always getting sick at reading time indicates that the program may need to be modified.

Teacher experience

Of course, experience tends to be the most crucial variable in evaluating performance data. From the experience of having taught other children similar skills, you will slowly acquire the "feel" for how long a child should spend learning each skill. By using ongoing assessment data, you add an objective measure to the subjective ability to "feel" when a child is experiencing difficulties. For the mildly handicapped student, the use of objective measures to determine satisfactory progress greatly enhances the probability of success.

The type of modification depends on whether the child is in the acquisition or the proficiency learning phase. Generally, if program modifications are required during the acquisition phase, teaching techniques need to be altered. When problems arise during the proficiency phasse, reinforcement or practice opportunities are altered. In all cases, the continued collection of ongoing assessment data determines the success of modification.

Modification during Acquisition

When deciding on possible modifications during acquisition, the first consideration should be: Has adequate time been allotted to determine if the procedure is effective? If the procedure has been given ample time and the child's progress is still unsatisfactory, you need to ask the following basic questions: First, is the goal appropriate? Did the child have the prerequisite entry skills to begin learning this skill? If the answer to this question is *no,* the teacher needs to establish a new long-term objective (see Figure 8.4). Second, are the steps in the sequence too large? Is the gap between the previous skill and the present target skill too big a step? If the answer to this question is *yes,* you will need to "slice back" and create smaller learning steps. Third, are the instructional procedures effective? You must closely examine the direct teacher instruction procedures, the opportunities for supervised practice, and the correctional feedback procedures. From this information, you select the most appropriate modified instructional techniques, implement the techniques, and continue to collect ongoing assessment data to verify if the modification is successful.

Behavior slicing

If you have determined that the steps in the teaching sequence were too large for the student, you will need to make the steps smaller. For the objective, "When given a topic, the child will write a five-sentence paragraph with a topic sentence and supportive details," a behavior slice might consist at first of only a single topic sentence. As we explained in Chapter 6, *behavior,* or *objective, slicing* simply refers to reducing the complexity or difficulty between the steps in the teaching sequence.

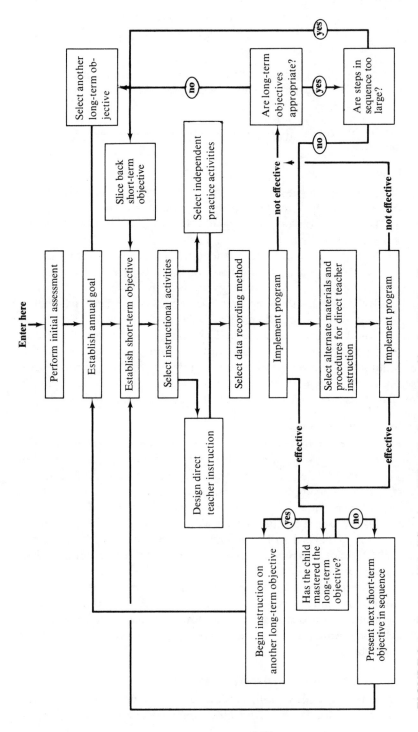

FIGURE 8.4. *Program Modifications When Program Is Ineffective During the Acquisition Stage*

Original target skill	*Possible behavior slicing*
Addition, facts, sums less than ten	Addition facts, sums less than four; less than eight; less than ten.
Spelling list of ten new words	Cumulative list of three new words at a time.
Answers literal comprehension questions demanding *who, what, when,* and *where.*	Answers literal comprehension questions when asked *who* questions.

By carefully reviewing the child's performance, you can determine how finely to "slice back" the objective.

Altering instructional procedures

The following questions and suggestions will help you evaluate and alter direct teacher instruction. Is the child attending to the instructions? Are the directions clear and concise? Is the instruction well organized? Select a term *(regrouping, renaming, borrowing)* and stick with that term. Can the visual stimuli be altered? In teaching CVCe words, perhaps color could be added to the vowels to further isolate the critical differences in the words. Could other modalities be stressed? Perhaps in learning to recognize syllables, rhythmical clapping could be added to the instruction. Could alternative demonstrations be used? In handwriting, perhaps demonstrating on the chalkboard is not specific enough; writing on the child's paper may be more effective. Would an alternative method of doing the skill work better? In teaching arithmetic, perhaps a different algorithm would improve student performance. Would another material work better? Perhaps changing from a basal reader to a programmed reader that elicits direct responses would increase comprehension. Above all else, ask the child, "What seems to be confusing you?"

Altering supervised practice of skills

Another area to be examined for possible modification are the various practice activities you use under close teacher supervision. Ask the following questions: Can additional prompts be used? "Before we start writing, the first word of each sentence is CAPITALIZED!" Could physical guidance be added? Guide a child's hand as she forms a letter. Were prompts faded—taken away—too quickly? The child was doing well in supervised practice of subtraction with renaming until the cross-out line, indicating which digit needed to be renamed, was removed. Is there enough supervised practice? Perhaps the practice activities are appropriate but the child does not have enough time to practice.

Error analysis will often provide you with the answers to the above questions. By carefully examining the child's errors, you should be able to determine exactly what part of the instructional process is breaking down. By using the technique of corrective feedback while watching the child perform the task, you will be able to redirect the child immediately.

Modification during Proficiency

Once a child has acquired a specific skill, practice is important until she becomes proficient in the skill. Practice and reinforcement appear to be the most effective

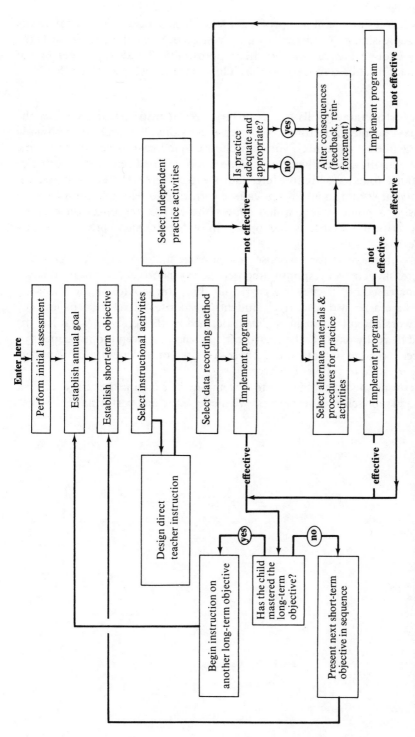

FIGURE 8.5. *Program Modifications When Program Is Ineffective During the Proficiency Stage*

techniques for increasing a skill to a proficient level. When a child in the proficiency phase is not progressing at a satisfactory rate, you need to ask the questions: Is the child receiving enough *appropriate* practice opportunities? Can reinforcement of child performance be altered to increase the child's proficiency? (See Figure 8.5.)

Practice

Drill and practice on target skills is a necessary part of instruction. Each day the child should have ample opportunity to increase her skills. By carefully examining the types of practice opportunities, you may choose to increase or decrease the time spent on these activities, alter them or provide a more varied selection of practice materials. Making practice activities into games often increases student participation. Both individuals and small groups can be formed into teams to compete with each other, using a point system which counts the correct responses on practice activities. The critical variable is the opportunity for frequent practice on appropriate materials.

Altering reinforcement for responses on practice material is a very effective method of increasing correct responses and decreasing incorrect responses. When a child has not increased proficiency in a particular skill, you should ask the following questions: Is there a reward to correct students' responses? Is there a payoff for doing correct work? Reinforcement is always defined by the receiver. What has the child indicated he really likes? Is the reinforcer too small or given too infrequently? Is the reinforcer too large so that the child becomes tired of it? Does the child understand what she must do to get the reinforcer?

These questions should enable you to systematically examine the reinforcement being given and to select alternatives whenever student performance is not satisfactory.

9

IMPLEMENTATION: GETTING YOUR PROGRAM TO WORK

ADAPTING FOR THE MILDLY HANDICAPPED STUDENT

We have discussed the necessity of individualizing instruction for the mildly handicapped child. This demands assessing individuals, setting goals, implementing instructional programming, and monitoring substantial deviance from peers in the academic areas of the classroom. However, these individual programs must be maintained within the structure of the regular classroom. In this final section we will discuss the implementation of this individualized programming.

Within the curriculum found in the elementary school there are three types of subject matter: *basic academic subjects* (math, spelling, reading, handwriting, language arts); *academic content areas* (science, social studies, health); and *nonacademic content areas* (art, music, physical education). Because of the similarities in instructional approaches usually used for these groupings of curriculum, each will be discussed in terms of adaptations needed for the mildly handicapped student.

Providing Instructional Adaptations in Basic Academic Subjects

Though the mildly handicapped student may be within the functioning levels of fellow students in one or more academic areas, he may be quite divergent in others. For those areas, alternate programs for the child must be created and carried out within the regular classroom.

The mildly handicapped child is easiest to accommodate in the classroom that has a totally individualized program, in which all children are given individually designed assignments and instruction. However, this type of classroom is a reality in

---

Anita Archer

only a few schools. Many attempts at total individualization have focused on providing individual, independent assignments and self-teaching materials while reducing the amount of direct teacher instruction. Mildly handicapped children usually need increased, not decreased, amounts of teacher instruction time and may not benefit from this type of individualization.

The majority of elementary classrooms utilize small-group instruction with supportive independent exercises. Because of the diversity of academic skills found within any regular classroom, small-group instruction is more appropriate than whole-group instruction for basic academic subjects. The diversity of skill levels necessitating small-group instruction is increased by the mainstreaming of mildly handicapped children within the regular classroom.

Small-group instruction in basic academic subjects

The challenge of small-group instruction for the mildly handicapped child is placement in the most appropriate instructional group. The first, and most desirable, option is to place the child in a homogenous group in which all children have the same entry skills and are working on the same instructional objective. Because the mildly handicapped child is often far below the class in specific academic areas, you may find homogenous placement impossible. However, options for homogenous groupings can be expanded with cross-grade and cross-class re-grouping in some schools.

The possibility of homogenous grouping can also be increased by the use of "skill-specific" groupings instead of "developmental" groupings (a group that has a consistent membership across the study of many skills). In skill-specific groupings, membership is more fluid and transient; membership in the group terminates when the skill is mastered. The groups are formed and reformed based on the instructional needs of the individual students within the classroom. For example, skill-specific groupings might be utilized for math. You could establish groups as certain children needed direct teacher instruction and supervised practice on a new skill. The skill-specific groupings might be initiated for instruction in telling time to the hour, regrouping in addition, or story problems with extraneous information included. When the children moved from the stage of initial acquisition to proficiency, the instructional group would terminate.

Skill-specific groups need not be formulated only for the purpose of in-troducing a new skill or concept; some of the group members could be selected in order to review or maintain a previously mastered skill. You may wish to introduce the concept of contractions to a mildly handicapped child in the fifth grade. If the teacher has noted inconsistent use of contractions and errors in forming them by three class members, then he includes them in the skill-specific group along with the handicapped pupil.

Though homogenous grouping is desirable, the skill level of the mildly handi-capped child may make this impossible. You can then consider a second option, heterogenous grouping. The mildly handicapped child could be placed in a group with children having a range of entry skills and varying short-term objectives. Within a small group, individualization on some skills is often possible. In a basal reading group, a teacher may have five children with different comprehension focuses: recall of detail, sequencing, main idea, critical analysis, and creative thinking. After reading a portion of the selection, the teacher may ask each child a specific question geared at his level of comprehension: "John, how many boys are in the story?"; "Sue, where did the boys go after they finished their lunch?"; "Charles, what would be a good title to the story?"; "Fred, do you think this story could actually have taken place?"; "Mark, how might you have solved the boy's problem?" This same type of individualization could occur in a skill-specific group organized to focus on word types (nouns, verbs, adverbs, adjectives). Though the instruction would be similar for all children, the types of examples given and the responses demanded from individual children could be varied. "Susan, is *house* a noun?"; "Charles, is *democracy* a noun?" Often you will be surprised by the "extraneous" or "incidental" information that the mildly handicapped child gains in a heterogenous grouping. The only caution in this type of grouping is to avoid confusing the mildly handicapped child by presenting information that interferes with learning a new concept.

A third option in placing a mildly handicapped child in an instructional group is to include the child in a heterogenous group that is focusing on a skill that is not a prime objective for the child. This should *never* be done as an alternative to individualized programming, but only as an extension of the child's classroom instruction or as an enrichment activity. When a child is placed in a heterogenous group on a nonindividualized objective, you should expect different responses and achievement from him. However, when carefully done, this can allow the child fuller participation within the classroom and less exclusion from peers. As already stated, the mildly handicapped child can often gain information from exposure to other skills and concepts. You might place a child in a skill-specific group organized to introduce outlining. Though the mildly handicapped child might not master all the skills involved, he may gain an idea of the difference between main ideas and supportive details, and the organization of outlines. Again, this is not an alternative to individualized programming, but an extension of the child's education. This option might be utilized when the mildly handicapped child needs close supervision and has few independent skills. You could include the child in nonindividualized groups and at the same time begin to build independent skills.

Individual instruction in basic academic areas

One-to-one instruction is often the most appropriate mode of instruction for the mildly handicapped child. Small-group instruction, even when using many possible options, may not provide enough direct teacher instruction for the mildly handicapped child. Individual time with a child need not come in large time segments; instruction can be organized into very short time periods. In three to five minutes you can introduce a new concept to a child and provide supervised practice; one or two minutes is often enough time to provide quality corrective feedback to a child. Individualized instruction must occur regularly at a consistent time each day. When individual instruction does not become a routine part of the day, it often becomes expendable. This can be avoided by having routine times for individual instruction to the mildly handicapped child.

Use of tutors and supportive professionals

You need to view your role as an "imparter of information" and as an instructional manager. To avoid shortchanging the mildly handicapped child, you can draw on many alternate sources for direct instruction. It can be given by classroom peers, an older child, an instructional aide, or a parent volunteer. Or it could be provided by professionals within the school: speech therapists, psychologists, reading teachers, and special educators. You should not exclude any possibilities when seeking help for the mildly handicapped child. Often, other professionals within the school, though not officially teachers, welcome the chance to work with individual children on a daily basis. Other possible assistants might be the school nurse, the office secretary, the principal, or the school librarian.

Tutors

When using instructional tutors whose prime role is not remediation of academic difficulties, you must take full responsibility for individual program planning. Determine the skills to be taught, the exact procedures to be used, and the exercises to be used with the child. Teachers sometimes find that it takes more time to give guidance to a tutor than to teach the child individually. However, by following certain procedures, the value of instruction from tutors can be increased and the time demanded by the teacher reduced.

You begin by designing a standard set of procedures to be used by the tutor. This should include a schedule of activities and procedures. The following procedures were developed for a high school tutor working with Kevin each day.

Step 1.   *Flash cards:* Show Kevin a flash card; if he responds incorrectly or slowly, place the card in the error pile.

Step 2.   *Practice of error cards:* Go through the error cards; give Kevin the problem orally; say the answer and have Kevin repeat the problem with the answer; repeat three times in this manner.

Step 3.   *Drill sheet:* Give Kevin the fact drill sheet; time him for one minute; correct his paper and graph the number of correct and incorrect responses.

Step 4.   *Math book:* Ask Kevin to complete three pages in a programmed math book.

Step 5.   *Math game:* Play one of the math fact games (Bingo, Concentration, Racetrack).

When first introducing the tutor to his role, it is helpful if the procedures to be used are carefully explained and demonstrated with the child. Though this will increase the amount of time you initially spend, it should reduce the problems the tutor may later face and increase the tutor's enjoyment by removing initial ambivalence concerning his duties.

The tutor's effectiveness is maximized when a definite method of communication is established between the tutor and the teacher. This can be a combination of written and verbal communication. The written communication can include data taken on performance, anecdotal comments concerning the day's activities, directions from you on procedures to use, and updated materials. A time for verbal communication needs to be established at least on a periodic basis.

The greatest difficulty with volunteer tutors is maintaining their commitment for a long period of time. There are ways, however, to improve the probability of their continued involvement. Some suggestions include: providing feedback, praise, and thanks for the tutor's efforts; allowing the tutor to take some responsibility in the programming for the child; and making the interaction with the child as positive as possible. In reinforcing the tutor for his efforts, you should give the tutor credit for the child's gains. Verbal praise and written notes given for both the student's and tutor's efforts will increase viability of the relationship. Tutors will be more consistent in coming and more enthusiastic about tutoring if they have some responsibility for program alterations within defined guidelines. To implement this idea, establish set rules for program modification that the tutor can follow: "When Tom gets the words right two days in a row, go down the list and select five new words." "When you feel the cover-copy-compare study method for the spelling words is no longer effective, you can select one of these alternate procedures." Tutors enjoy making decisions, but are often frustrated when firm guidelines are not established.

As a general rule, the tutor will enjoy his interaction with the child if the *child* finds the interaction pleasant and profitable. You can effectively manipulate the types of subject matter and activities to increase the probability of mutual enjoyment of the experience. First, select a subject area for the tutoring sessions that the child enjoys. A balance of fun activities can be included in planning tutor sessions. For example, in the previous description of a math session, the teacher programmed a game at the end of the session. Other simple activities can be added that increase the child's interest in the tutoring sessions: use of the stopwatch; inclusion of media (tape recorder); use of games or graphing of data. You can train the tutor in the effective use of reinforcers. For example, the tutor could add a star to a chart, send a note to the teacher on days of good performance, make the final game contingent on a certain performance, or have the child work for a special object or for access to a special event during the tutoring session.

You must be available for assistance if the tutor has difficulty in behavior management. Particularly when using volunteer tutors, behavior problems can arise. These tutors do not have "authority" over the child's behavior except as authorized by you. Because of their role within the school environment, you must maintain your involvement in the interaction so that the child realizes that your behavioral expectations and authority continue within the tutoring sessions. Potential behavior and discipline problems can be reduced when: tutoring takes place within the classroom; the teacher intermittently enters the tutoring session; communication is open and continuous between the tutor and the teacher. It may also be necessary to teach the tutor specific methods of behavioral management: the setting of clear, consistent behavioral expectations (rules); the use of consistent routines; the use of reinforcement following desired behaviors; and the use of ignoring as a management technique.

Peers

Because of their availability in any classroom setting, peers are excellent sources of direct instructional tutoring. One of the more effective pairings consists of a pupil who is at the stage of initial acquisition on a skill and a peer tutor who is at the stage of proficiency. This gives the learner valuable instruction, and provides needed practice for the tutor. Tutors can also be paired for reciprocal tutoring. For example, Sam could drill Sandy on her addition facts with sums to ten (a skill Sam has mastered) and Sandy could in turn drill Sam on his twelve spelling words.

Use of other professionals

The regular classroom teacher should avail himself of all services offered by support professionals (special educators, speech therapists, reading teachers) whose specific role is remediation of academic difficulties. These professionals will often use the systematic instructional procedures described in this chapter. Duplication of efforts can be avoided by utilizing services of support professionals.

However, you must take an active role in the child's remedial program even when maintained by another individual. As a regular classroom teacher, you have daily interaction with the child and, as a result, have valuable information to contribute to program planning. Setting goals should be a joint process between specialist and teacher. You should combine your daily experience, knowledge of the child's classroom performance, and assessment information with the specialist's diagnostic information to form the most appropriate objectives for the child.

It is of prime importance that communication between the teacher and the specialist be maintained. You must know what skills the child is learning in order to reinforce these skills on a continual basis. Likewise, the specialist needs to continually update the child's goals and objectives in response to the demands of the regular classroom, and later update the child's program to reflect current needs. The classroom teacher and the specialist must maintain communication to ensure that there are consistent behavioral patterns and performance of skills across settings.

There are many ways that this sharing of information in a cooperative program can occur:

1. The specialist and teacher can communicate casually over lunch or during recess duty.

2. They can communicate on a scheduled, formalized basis.

3. They can jointly conference with parents to share information on the child's total remedial program.

4. The specialist can work with the child in the classroom.

5. The classroom teacher can examine the child's work completed with the specialist on a regular basis.

6. The child can independently complete assignments from the specialist during independent sessions in the classroom.

All of these methods can be used to open and maintain communication concerning the child's performance and goals.

When a child leaves the classroom to work with a reading teacher, resource room teacher, or speech therapist, he will usually be working on skills of his greatest deficiency. To maximize the child's success within the regular classroom, you can schedule the subjects of greatest difficulty for the child while he is at his special remedial sessions. For example, John is a mildly handicapped child in fourth grade. Though he functions quite well in math, he is two years deficient in reading. Each day, John leaves the classroom to work for an hour in the resource room on reading skills. This same period of time is used for reading within the regular classroom. When John returns, reading is completed and activities in which he will have more success are scheduled.

Programming independent work in basic academic areas

A portion of the child's day is usually spent on independent activities. Many of the mildly handicapped child's assignments will differ from his peers because he is working on alternate skills. In selecting independent assignments for this child, you must first consider the objectives the child is working on that are beyond the stage of initial acquisition. You must then make special provisions to increase the mildly handicapped child's ability to independently complete assignments. Standard formats reduce the need for special directions. You can also introduce new assignments during instruction. You might increase independence in these ways:

1. Put the child's direction on tapes.

2. Establish a regular routine for the child to follow.

3. Place the child's work in a folder indicating the order of desired completion.

4. Establish a plan sheet for the child to follow which would direct the child to complete certain activities. This type of plan sheet could also be used by the child to check off completed assignments and to record daily data (see Table 9.1).

TABLE 9.1

Assignment Sheet and Record of Completion for Kraig

Name Kraig Check assignments off as completed.									
	Monday		Tuesday		Wednesday		Thursday		Friday
Science Research Associates Lab	Orange 4	✓	Orange 5	✓	Orange 6	✓	Orange 6	✓	Orange 7	✓
Skill Workbook	Page 19	✓	Page 21	✓	Page 22/23	✓	Page 25	✓	Page 26	✓
Comprehension Questions (file)	#8	✓	#12	✓	#10	✓	#15	✓	#11	✓
Language Master Cards		✓		✓		✓		✓		✓

NOTE: This assignment sheet was designed for use by Kraig, a mildly handicapped child in the fifth grade. Kraig's independent-child interventions were substantially different from others in the classroom. Kraig used this sheet to determine what assignments to complete and the order of completion. As he finished a task, Kraig checked it off and proceeded to the next task.

You should consider taping directions to provide a possible expansion of direct teacher instructional time. The mildly handicapped child often needs more instruction on a particular skill before mastery occurs, and tapes can be effectively used for this purpose. For example, following introduction of the phoneme-grapheme relationship of *oi*, the teacher could prepare an instructional tape to review this concept. Using a worksheet from a phonics book, the teacher could remind the child of a new sound, go through sample exercises with the child, guide the child in completion of items, and provide feedback on correct answers. Tape recorders and language masters can adapt to many special programming needs: spelling lists can be placed on language master cards; creative writing assignments can be explained to the child on a tape; and basal reading vocabulary can be reinforced using the tape recorder.

Providing Instructional Adaptations in Academic Content Areas

When teaching science, social studies, health, and current events, the teacher has many options for providing instruction, including lectures, discussions, films, filmstrips, classroom projects, and experiments. In addition to these methods, the content area textbook is commonly used. The mildly handicapped child who has deficient reading skills has difficulty learning when the prime source of instruction is the content textbook. The child may gain the information and concepts when presented orally; but he may be unable to process information presented in written form. If you wish to use the textbook to present information, there are options that allow the mildly handicapped child to participate: the classroom members can orally read the material; you can read the material to the class; a peer or volunteer can read the material to the child; or the material can be taped for the child to listen to during instructional periods when other children are reading independently. You can also provide an alternate text on the subject written at the child's independent reading level, either content area texts covering the same information at a lower grade level or a library book on the subject. To reduce the stigma attached to reading lower grade level books, you should select content area texts that the children are not familiar with and that have no external markings of grade level. Another option is to rewrite the class material into a simpler format. For the teacher serving many children deficient in reading over a number of years, this would be a valuable type of material to develop. Rewriting materials and taping content texts can be done by enthusiastic volunteers and willing parents.

When reading *must* be the major form of instruction in content areas, the mildly handicapped child may experience difficulty. Likewise, when a written response (e.g., essay answers, paragraphs) is demanded, the mildly handicapped child may have difficulty responding. You should provide alternate ways of responding such as oral responses, discussion groups, projects, or displays. In geography, for example, the children could draw maps or complete models of globes. The mildly handicapped child may perform with more ease on this type of task. These projects are also easily adapted to small group participation, enabling further involvement in classroom activities by the mildly handicapped child.

While providing alternate responses, you may also desire the completion of written assignments, completion of chapter or unit questions in content text, or the writing of a report. The mildly handicapped child may have difficulty on these assignments because of the reading level of the questions, the written response demands, and the complexity of the questions. You can reduce the difficulty of written assignments by rewording questions, altering the response demanded, and reducing the amount of writing needed to complete the answer. In the following example the teacher has restructured this question from a social studies book to allow the child to make a word or phrase answer. The question has also been re-worded to include only the child's "decodable" vocabulary.

> *Question from text.* "Name three ways that the Eskimo culture has adapted to the habitat of Alaska."
> *Restructured question:*
> The Eskimos eat _____
> The clothes of the Eskimo are made from _____
> The houses of the Eskimo are made of _____

Students in intermediate grades are often required to write reports on topics studied in the academic content areas. The mildly handicapped child may have difficulty in reading the necessary material, organizing the material, and in writing the report. The child could use a simple outline designed by the teacher. The child researches the topic using low reading level materials, lower grade level content materials, film strips, and slides; fills out the outline; and finally translates his outline into simple sentences or paragraphs (see Table 9.2). You will often find that materials developed for the mildly handicapped child, such as alternate written questions, taped textbooks, and report outline forms, are also useful with the marginal child who struggles with classroom assignments.

TABLE 9.2

Example Outline for Social Studies Report

I. Name of state: _____
  A. History and symbols
    1. Year became state: _____
    2. State bird: _____
    3. State flower: _____
    4. State flag (draw on separate sheet of paper).
  B. Location of state
    1. _____ is in the _____ (north, south, east, west).
    2. Bordering states: _____ , _____ ,
      _____ , _____ , _____ .
    3. State map (draw on separate sheet of paper).
  C. Physical features
    1. Name of mountains: _____
      _____ .
    2. Name of rivers: _____
      _____ .
    3. Name of lakes: _____
      _____ .
  D. Cities in state
    1. Largest city: _____
    2. Capital city: _____

TABLE 9.2 *Example Outline for Social Studies Report (cont.)*

E. People

    1. Population (how many people) _____

    2. Jobs many people do: _____

        _____

    3. Special things people do for fun: _____

        _____

F. Major crops grown

    1. _____

    2. _____

    3. _____

G. Major industries in state

    1. _____

        _____

    2. _____

        _____

    3. _____

        _____

Providing Instructional Adaptations in Nonacademic Content Areas

Fewer adaptations are usually needed by the mildly handicapped child for successful participation in the nonacademic content areas of art, music, and physical education, due to a wider range of acceptable performance. Even with minimal skills, the mildly handicapped child can actively participate if you provide careful instructions, ensure that the child can complete the project, and, finally, maintain consistent management of behavior.

A mildly handicapped child may have difficulty following directions given for an art project, music activity, or physical activity. To increase the effectiveness of directions, you should command all of the children's attention, use simple verbal directions, and accompany the verbal directions with demonstration when possible. The mildly handicapped child can be placed next to a more able child during P.E., music, or art activities for additional prompts on the responses demanded.

In a few cases, the teacher may have to slightly alter the response demands to allow full participation by the mildly handicapped child. In art class, for example, a portion of the project might be completed by the teacher (cutting out small parts). In physical education, the teacher can allow a range of acceptable performance that encourages all to participate. She might direct, "Run around the gym at least once. Continue until I blow my whistle or until you become tired." This type of direction would allow even the less able child to participate.

Behaviors often deteriorate during art, music, and physical education. This is probably due to the change from routine, the alterations of behavioral expectations, and the change in the classroom setting. The mildly handicapped child, particularly the child with behavioral disorders, may have difficulty coping with total change in behavioral expectations and the additional freedom allowed in these activites. To reduce the probability of behavior problems you should:

1. Introduce consistent rules to cover behaviors in this situation.
2. Structure the environment to encourage desired behaviors.
3. Maintain specific contingencies for desired classroom behavior during these activities.

CREATING A POSITIVE LEARNING ENVIRONMENT FOR ALL CHILDREN

The classroom should be a pleasant and productive environment for all children. This means that every child must be aware of the teacher's expectations; must understand classroom rules and routines; feel included in the classroom activities; and experience success.

Expectations and Consistency

Teacher expectations are made explicit by the use of a few concrete classroom rules that are clearly stated each day. Consistent routines allow the students to predict forthcoming activities. When children know what is expected of them and what activities are going to take place, they are more confident of performing with success. This does not mean that you should be so inflexible that you ignore special "teachable moments." When the birth of a new baby sister opens the door for a class discussion of where babies come from, or a television special touches the interests of the entire class, teachers should be ready and willing to capitalize on these events to discuss new areas of learning. However, standard procedures provide children with a feeling of security—the ability to predict what is going to happen next—and thus enables them to perform at optimum levels.

Including All Children in Activities

Classrooms should be places where children are given the opportunity to learn and practice new academic and social behaviors. This idea demands group activities. During each day a portion of the classroom time is used for total class participation. Activities during this time may be as simple as a show and tell period or as complex as a class meeting to resolve a problem. Whatever the case, all the children must be included in the activity. You must make special efforts to include the children who are not participating by asking specific children questions, reinforcing comments from children who rarely respond, not tolerating scapegoating, and most important, modeling for all the students how to accept each other as individuals. In group games, make sure that all the children have an equal opportunity to succeed; often this means the use of different types of questions for some of the students.

There are times during the typical school day when subgroups of the class work together on projects. A perceptive teacher will carefully form these subgroups to facilitate grouping across academic levels whenever possible. The formation of subgroups avoids the labeling of fast or slow groups, the smart ones or the dumb ones, the "eagles" or the "sparrows." Children of varied academic ability can function together as a group; the careful grouping of students in these activities does much to give all children the feeling of belonging to the entire group. By crossing academic level grouping whenever possible, you can enrich the classroom environment for each student. Children who always work by themselves on "baby stuff" do not contribute to a positive atmosphere in any classroom. These children develop a dislike for school that adversely affects their academic performance and that feeds the cycle of poor work leading to poor self concept, which further promotes poor work.

Ensuring Success

Each individual, in order to grow, must experience accomplishment. Going to school for children can be equated to going to work for adults. No one feels good or performs well when she experiences failure after failure. By carefully assessing children's skills, providing instructional material that is appropriate for each child, reinforcing correct performance, altering the instructional plan when needed, and involving all the children in regular classroom activities as much as possible, you will help ensure success for all children. When children succeed in a friendly, warm environment, they feel good about themselves and their surroundings, which is what school is all about.

Appendix

CASE STUDY: JOE

The following case study illustrates the concepts of and the procedures for implementing systematic instruction for the mildly handicapped child within the regular classroom, which we have presented in the last seven chapters.

Background

Joe is a six-year-old boy who entered first grade from a kindergarten class in the same school district. Joe's initial skills and interaction in the first-grade classroom prompted his new teacher to seek additional information on Joe to substantiate a possible referral to the special services committee within the school. Mr. Thomas, the first-grade teacher, began by talking with the kindergarten teacher about Joe's performance concerning readiness skills and ability to follow directions. The kindergarten teacher reported that Joe frequently wandered around the classroom, could not name or write letters and numerals, and had difficulty with fine-motor and self-help skills, such as cutting paper and putting on his coat. Following discussions with Joe's former teacher, further observations of Joe within a variety of classroom activities and substantiating observations made by the school counselor, Mr. Thomas formally referred Joe to the Special Services Committee for a complete evaluation of Joe's specific instructional needs to determine his eligibility for special services.

Assessment

The Special Services Committee reviewed the referral and accompanying information, determined that assessment was needed in the areas of academic achievement (readiness skills and early academics), intellectual functioning, school behaviors, and language and communication. A letter was written to Mr. and Mrs. Martin, Joe's parents, explaining the nature of the referral from Mr. Thomas recommending formal evaluation, discussing the evaluation procedures that would be followed, and listing their parental rights. They were also informed about what would happen to Joe depending on the outcome of the formal evaluation (e.g., if it was determined that Joe was eligible for special services, an IEP committee would be established, and Joe's parents would be involved in formulating an individual education program for Joe). In addition, Mr. Thomas asked the Martins to come to a parent conference to discuss Joe's classroom performance and to provide them with further information concerning the referral to the special services committee.

Within the same week, the consent to proceed with formal evaluation was received from Mr. and Mrs. Martin and the chairperson of the special services committee assigned four staff members to the multidisciplinary committee to evaluate Joe: the speech therapist, the school psychologist, the special education resource room teacher, and Mr. Thomas. Each team member agreed to assess specific areas of functioning and to write formal evaluation reports within two weeks. The school psychologist administered two tests of intellectual functioning, the Wechsler Preschool and Primary Scale of Intelligence (Wechsler, 1967) and the Pictorial Test of Intelligence (French, 1964). In addition, the school psychologist observed Joe in the classroom for five half-hour periods, taking data on out-of-seat behavior and making informal notations concerning other school behaviors such as attending to the teacher, following directions, and locating school supplies. The speech therapist administered the Boehm Test of Basic Concepts and informal tests of direction following, and took language samples of Joe's expressive language. The resource room teacher administered informal tests of reading readiness (e.g., saying isolated sounds, matching letters, blending oral sounds into words, and segmenting oral words into sounds). Mr. Thomas administered the readiness subtests of the Brigance Diagnostic Inventory of Basic Skills (Brigance, 1977) to Joe. (Mr. Thomas's evaluation report is found in Table A-1.)

Upon completion of the formal evaluation and writing of the evaluation reports, the multidisciplinary team met and reviewed all of the testing information. Based on the evaluation results, the team members determined that Joe was eligible for special education services and could be classified as mildly retarded under the state guidelines. It was agreed that the Martins should be informed of the evaluation results, of the eligibility of their son for special services, and of the scheduling of an IEP conference both through a letter and a personal conference. Within the letter informing Mr. and Mrs. Martin of the test results, they were asked to come to a parent conference with the first-grade teacher and the school psychologist to discuss the evaluation results and the future development of an IEP for Joe. At the parent conference, Mr. Thomas reviewed the evaluation results collected by him; the resource room teacher and the speech therapist reviewed Joe's academic functioning, stressing his strengths as well as areas of need. The school psychologist reviewed the intellectual assessment results, again with an emphasis on Joe's strengths and weaknesses rather than on test scores. After a discussion of the test results and the Martins' questions concerning their son's performance, Mr. Thomas described parent involvement in the IEP process, and scheduled an IEP conference with Joe's parents.

TABLE A-1

Evaluation Report

Name: Joe Martin   *Teacher:* Robert Thomas
Date of birth: June 4, 1972   *Test administrator:* Mr. Thomas
Age: 6   *Test Administered:* Brigance Diagnostic
School: Park Elementary School   Inventory of Basic Skills:
Grade: 1st   Readiness subtest

Background information:

Joe Martin was referred to the special services committee by his classroom teacher, Mr. Thomas, because of his low performance on basic academic tasks within the first weeks of first grade and reports from his kindergarten teacher concerning performance during his first year of school.

Test results:

Joe was administered the readiness subtests on the Brigance Diagnostic Inventory of Basic Skills, a criterion-referenced assessment tool. The following information summarizes Joe's performance on each of the subtests.

Subtest	*Strengths*	*Weaknesses*
Color recognition	Can name colors red and blue	Cannot name other basic colors
Visual discrimination	Can match basic shapes and letters	Has difficulty matching very similar letters and short words
Visual-motor skills	Can copy simple shapes	Cannot accurately copy complex shapes
Visual memory	Can draw single shapes from memory	Has difficulty drawing a series of shapes from memory
Body image	Includes basic body parts when asked to draw a person	Does not include details in drawing (e.g., facial features, fingernails)
Body parts	Can identify majority of body parts	Can not identify shoulder, knee, hip, ankle, elbow, or wrists
Directional/positional skills	Understands majority of concepts	Does not respond correctly to *beneath, beside, forward, backward, next to*
Fine motor skills	Can put on his coat, button coat, and open and close zipper	Cannot lace or tie shoes Has difficulty using scissors
Verbal fluency	Responds verbally with phrases	Seldom uses complete sentences or questions; ideas not always related
Verbal directions	Can follow one direction	Has difficulty with a series of directions
Articulation of sounds	Produces the majority of sounds correctly in initial position of words	Has difficulty articulating *f, j, wh, s, th,* and *sh*
Personal data response	Can tell his first name, age, and address	Does not tell full name, telephone number, birthday, and parents' names
Sentence memory	Can repeat sentences of 2 to 4 syllables	Has difficulty repeating longer sentences
Counting	Rote counts to 5	Will not continue beyond
Alphabet	Says the alphabet through *d.*	No response after d

TABLE A-1 *Evaluation Report (Con't)*

Number recognition	Points correctly to numerals 1 and 2	Random responses
Number comprehension	Can indicate correct number of fingers for 1 and 2	Will not attempt numbers after 2
Recognition of lower case letters	Correctly identifies *a* and *c*	Unsure on remaining letters
Recognition of upper case letters	Correctly identifies *J*	Unsure on remaining letters
Writing name	Can write his first name	Unable to write last name
Lower case letters by dictation		Unable to write any of the letters
Upper case letters by dictation.	Can write the letter *J*	Unable to write any of the remaining letters

Summary: During the test administration, Joe was very attentive and tried all of the tasks. He was quite aware of the information he knew and did not know. If the information was not known, he generally informed the teacher rather than attempting the task. Though he has gained some readiness skills such as writing his first name, counting to 5, and following simple directions, he has difficulty with many of the skills expected of entering first graders.

Recommendations: Because of the substantial discrepancy between Joe's skills and those of his classmates, he is in need of specialized instruction in the basic academic areas of reading, math, and handwriting. In addition, Joe needs to be taught basic concepts such as colors and shapes. There is some indication that Joe will also need consistent instruction in language as indicated by his difficulty in following verbal directions, repeating sentences from memory, responding to basic concepts, and responding verbally at the same level of maturity as his peers. Further assessment in this area should be made by the speech therapist.

Development of Individualized Education Program

After the evaluating team had determined Joe's eligibility for special education and related services, the head of the Special Services Committee appointed members to the IEP committee. Although initially this committee need include only one member from the evaluation team, all four members were assigned to the IEP committee since they were likely to work with Joe depending on where he was placed. In addition, Joe's parents and school principal became members of the IEP committee.

Though there are a number of ways to proceed, the committee members decided to divide the responsibility of writing preliminary drafts of portions of the IEP. The committee members met, reviewed the evaluation data available on Joe, determined areas of greatest need, and assigned development of preliminary goals and objectives to various team members. For example, the resource room teacher was given primary responsibility for reading, Mr. Thomas for math, the speech therapist for expressive and receptive verbal language, and the parents for self-help skills.

One week later, at the beginning of the second meeting of the committee, the chairperson introduced all team members, and established an overview of the meeting and the tasks that were to be completed. Following this introduction, Mrs. Johnson, the chairperson, asked team members to state areas in which they believed Joe needed special services beyond the instructional program generally provided within the first-grade classroom. Areas were identified and written on the board. When all areas of need were identified and agreed upon, team members who had focused on specific areas presented preliminary drafts of an IEP. Each member briefly described Joe's current functioning level, suggested annual goals and short-term objectives, and solicited input from other team members concerning the appropriateness and priorities of the goals. The staff members were particularly careful to avoid educational jargon and to involve the parents in the discussion. When all of the goals and objectives had been reviewed and revised, the committee determined the levels of special education and related services necessary for carrying out the goals and objectives. The committee members agreed that Joe could participate in many of the first-grade activities though specialized instruction by the resource room teacher and the speech therapist would be necessary to maximize his progress. One and one-half hours of instruction in the resource room was planned with an additional half-hour of services provided each day by the speech therapist. After determining placement for Joe, responsibility for implementing instruction was assigned to three of the team members: the speech therapist, the regular classroom teacher, and the resource room teacher. Prior to the close of the meeting, all committee members signed the IEP, indicating that they believed it to represent an appropriate educational program for Joe. Table A-2 includes segments of the IEP developed for Joe. (See pages 168–71.)

Selection of Interventions and Data Recording Method

Following selection of short-term objectives, Mr. Thomas decided on interventions to be used when introducing each new skill during direct teacher instruction, and practice activities to be used upon initial acquisition. Mr. Thomas also established a method for collecting and recording data on each of the short-term objectives. Below are Mr. Thomas's plans for one objective:

Rote Counting:
Direct teacher instruction: I will model rote counting, and Joe will repeat. We will rote count together and alternately.
Peer tutor: Joe will work with James each day, clapping and rote counting in unison and independently.
Independent child activities: Instructional tapes will direct Joe through rote counting exercises.
Measurement activity: At the beginning of the instructional period, Joe will be asked to count as high as he can. The last number will be recorded on a graph.

Classroom Organization

In the mornings, Mr. Thomas used a rotating group organizational model. Opening activities were followed by a sixty-minute math period, divided into four fifteen-minute time segments. The children were grouped into four small groups for math instruction. They rotated as small groups to four areas in the room: *group table* for direct teacher instruction, *listening post* (taped instruction), *manipulative math*

TABLE A-2

Portions of the IEP written for Joe

Student: Joe Martin
Subject area: Math
Teacher: Thomas

Level of Performance: Can rote count to five. Can identify numerals one and two. Can count sets having one or two members. Cannot write any numerals. Cannot perform any math operations.

Annual goals	Short-term objectives	Date achieved	Person responsible
When asked to count, Joe will rote count to 20.	When asked to count, Joe will rote count to 10 correctly for three consecutive trials.		Thomas
	When asked to count, Joe will rote count to 15 correctly for three consecutive trials.		
	When asked to count, Joe will rote count to 20 correctly for three consecutive trials.		
When shown a card with a printed numeral (1 to 10), Joe will name numeral.	When shown cards with numerals 1, 2, and 3, Joe will correctly name the numerals.		Thomas
	When shown cards with numerals 1 to 4, Joe will correctly name the numerals.		
	When shown cards with numerals 1 to 5, Joe will correctly name the numerals.		
	Same objective for: 1-6 1-7 1-8 1-9 1-10		

Note: Numerals will be presented in random order.

Annual goals	Short-term objectives	Date achieved	Person responsible
When given a set with 1 to 10 members, Joe will count the number of members in the set.	When given a set with 1 to 3 members, Joe will count the number of members in the set correctly for three trials.		Thomas
	When given a set with 1 to 4 members, Joe will count the number of members in the set correctly for three trials.		
	Same objective for: 1-5 1-6 1-7 1-8 1-9 1-10		
When dictated the numeral name, Joe can accurately write the numeral.	When dictated the numerals 1 and 2, Joe will accurately write the numerals.		Thomas
	When dictated the numerals 1, 2 and 3, Joe will accurately write the numerals.		
	When dictated the numerals 1, 2, 3, and 4, Joe will accurately write the numerals.		
	Same objective for: 1-5 1-6 1-7 1-8 1-9 1-10		

169

TABLE A-2
Math IEP *(cont.)*

Annual goals	Short-term objectives	Date achieved	Person responsible
When given 10 addition facts with sums 1 to 10, Joe can write the sums with 100% accuracy.	When given 10 addition facts with addends of one and sums no greater than 10 (e.g., $5 + 1 = \quad, 6 + 1 = \quad, 7 + 1 = \quad$), Joe will write the sums with 100% accuracy.		Thomas
	Same objective: Addend of 2, sums to 10 Addend of 3, sums to 10 Addend of 4, sums to 10 Addend of 5, sums to 10 (Note: Inverse facts taught at same time. $6 + 1 = \quad 1 + 6 =$).		

Student: Joe Martin
Subject area: Reading
Teacher: Thomas

Level of Performance: Can read his name. Does not know any letter sounds.

Annual goals	Short-term objectives	Date achieved	Person responsible
Readiness Skills			
When presented a word, Joe will be able to segment into phonemes (e.g., teacher says cat. Joe says /c/ /a/ /t/).	When presented a word including 2 sounds, Joe will say the word by sounds (/a/ /t/).		Johnson
	When presented a word including 3 sounds, Joe will say the word by sounds (/p/ /a/ /t/).		
	When presented a word including 4 sounds, Joe will say the word by sounds (/b/ /r/ /a/ /t/).		
When presented isolated sounds, Joe will be able to blend the sounds into a word (e.g., teacher says /c/ /a/ /t/. Joe says cat).	When presented two sounds in isolation, Joe will blend the sounds into a word (e.g., at).		Johnson
	Same objective: 3 sounds 4 sounds		
When presented with a model word, Joe will produce rhyming words when given a new initial sound. (e.g., Teacher says "We are rhyming with at. B." Joe says "bat.")	When presented with a model word, Joe will produce rhyming words when given a new initial sound correctly in 10 of 10 trials.		Johnson

NOTE: The first four annual goals will be worked on concurrently. When Joe can count to a specific number, object counting will be introduced. When he can count a set of objects to a certain number, reading and writing of the numeral will be introduced. When Joe can count objects to 10, read numerals to 10 and write numerals to 10, addition facts to 10 will be introduced.

171

area, and *individual desks* for paper-and-pencil tasks. The work was the same for all members of the small group at the listening post, but differed between members at the paper-and-pencil tasks and manipulative math work area (see Table A-3).

TABLE A-3

Physical Arrangement of Joe's First- Grade Classroom

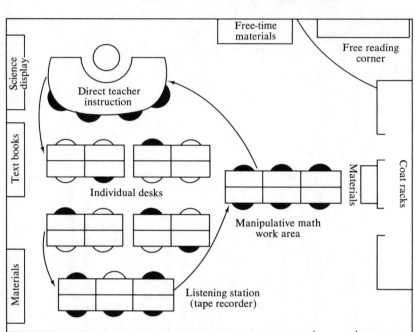

NOTE: This table illustrates the physical organization of Joe's classroom during math period. The children were grouped in four small groups, each beginning the instructional period at a different work area. Every fifteen minutes (when Mr. Thomas rang a bell) the children moved to the next area. Arrows indicate movement of small groups between direct-teacher instruction table, desks, listening station, and manipulative math area.

After recess, the children returned to the classroom for one hour of reading instruction. Mr. Thomas used the same rotating group organization for instruction in reading. Every fifteen minutes, Mr. Thomas, who was stationed at the group table, would ring a bell telling the children in the classroom to move to their next work areas. As soon as all of the children were seated, Mr. Thomas would provide direct teacher instruction to a small group. The four work areas in the class during reading were paper-and-pencil seatwork, taped instruction (listening post), free reading corner, and direct teacher instruction. At the end of the reading period the children would return to their seats and would listen to a story read by Mr. Thomas followed by oral comprehension questions to the children.

To facilitate the use of a rotating instructional group model, Mr. Thomas recruited sixth-grade tutors to help during these periods. The tutors had to earn this privilege by completing their work before they could help teach the first graders. The tutors monitored the students who were working independently, providing feedback on their work. They paid special attention to Joe's group which was the lowest performing group.

Handwriting was a whole-group activity in which each child worked at his own level, completing handwriting assignments at his desk. Mr. Thomas rotated among the children providing instruction on new letters and corrective feedback on performance.

In the afternoons, Mr. Thomas had art activities, social studies, and science. Twice a week the children left the room to go to physical education and music. Once a week the children went to the library. Presented here is the daily schedule used in the classroom (see Table A-4).

TABLE A-4

Daily Schedule for Joe's Classroom

8:45   Opening activities (whole group)

9:00   Math period (small groups)

	Group A	Group B	Group C	Group D
9:00	Group table	Manipulative tasks	Tape recorder	Paper-pencil tasks
9:15	Paper-pencil tasks	Group table	Manipulative tasks	Tape recorder
9:30	Tape recorder	Paper-pencil tasks	Group table	Manipulative tasks
9:45	Manipulative tasks	Tape recorder	Paper-pencil tasks	Group table

10:00   Recess

10:15   Reading (small group)

	Group 1	Group 2	Group 3	Group 4
10:15	Group table	Free reading center	Tape recorder	Paper-pencil tasks
10:30	Paper-pencil tasks	Group table	Free reading center	Tape recorder
10:45	Tape recorder	Paper-pencil tasks	Group table	Free reading center
11:00	Free reading center	Tape recorder	Paper-pencil tasks	Group table

11:15   Story time (whole group)

11:30   Handwriting (whole group with corrective feedback from teacher)

11:45   Lunch

12:30   Science or social studies activities

1:00   Physical education or music

1:30   Art activity or "Electric Company"

2:15   School out

Implementation of Joe's Program in Ongoing Classroom Activities

Joe was able to actively participate in the opening activities of the day. He shared responsibilities (watering the flowers, taking the lunch count to the kitchen) with other children in the classroom. Mr. Thomas assisted Joe during show and tell by previewing the show and tell with Joe—helping him decide what was important to say and how to say it so that the other children would understand.

Because of Joe's divergence from the class in all academic areas, Mr. Thomas scheduled Joe's sessions with specialists during classroom academic sessions. Joe received special reading instruction during the first thirty minutes of reading group and speech therapy for fifteen minutes during the math period.

When Joe returned to the class for the last forty-five minutes of math, he joined the lowest group, which had only four members. Since Joe was far behind his classmates in counting, Mr. Thomas arranged for Joe to work in counting with a peer tutor. At the manipulative station, Joe completed a variety of manipulative tasks involving simple counting. For example, Joe might count the beans in a cupcake holder and add a piece of paper with the numeral for the set. At the end of the manipulative station time the peer tutor would work with Joe. The peer tutor would clap and count to ten and have Joe count after him. The children would then clap and count in unison, followed by reciprocal counting. At the beginning of the fifteen minute direct teacher instruction, Mr. Thomas would take data on the objectives the four children were presently working on. Joe would be asked to count as high as he could, name numerals, write numerals, and count sets of objects. This probing for the purpose of ongoing assessment took the first five minutes of the direct teacher instructional period. Because of the heterogenous makeup of the small math group, Mr. Thomas had the children tutor each other on different activities while he introduced new skills to the other children. The children played games in math group that allowed individual practice of current objectives. After direct teacher instruction, Joe went to his seat and completed his paper-and-pencil tasks, including practice in writing numerals, counting sets, and writing numerals in serial order.

Joe was far more deficient in reading. He had not yet acquired even the most basic reading readiness skills. Mr. Thomas referred Joe to the reading specialist in the school for instruction each day. Joe went to the reading teacher immediately after recess and returned thirty minutes later. He then joined a direct teacher instructional period focusing on letter naming.

Joe was in a heterogenous reading group with three other children. Mr. Thomas spent five minutes asking the various children to name the letters he held up. During this time, Mr. Thomas pointed out the differences among the various letters and asked the children to do the same. Following this exercise, each child worked on language master cards, where they named the letter on the card and then listened to hear if they were correct. Finally, a tutor from the sixth grade took a one-minute sample of the children responding to flash cards with the letters they were learning. Mr. Thomas kept a record of the student responses in the one-minute sample. The tutors practiced the correct answers to all the problems that the students had missed. For each letter learned, the child received a smiling face sticker.

Following the reading group, Joe went to his desk and completed reading readiness paper-and-pencil tasks. Joe brought back to the classroom two of the sheets provided each day by the reading teacher. The other assignments included writing letters, writing names, and "fun" readiness worksheets to be done when he completed the other sheets in his folder.

During reading time, Mr. Thomas always read a story to all of the children. At the end of the story, he posed questions to the children about the story. For Joe, Mr. Thomas always asked questions requiring a two-word sentence, a noun and a verb. ("Joe, what did Sally do when she saw the bear?"). If Joe did not answer the question with two words, a noun and a verb, Mr. Thomas modeled the correct response. ("*Sally ran*. Joe, you say '*Sally ran*.' ") Mr. Thomas praised Joe for all correct responses. Correct and incorrect responses for each child were kept on a two-column sheet labeled *yes* and *no* for this activity.

No special adaptations were made for Joe during handwriting, since this activity was individualized for all children. The children were given a worksheet to practice letter or numeral formation. The teacher would circulate around the room providing corrective feedback on performance. Mr. Thomas was careful to provide extra attention to Joe at this time. He stressed not only the writing of the letters but also the naming of the letter as he worked with Joe at his desk.

The only additional reinforcement program that Mr. Thomas used to help Joe in his school work involved the boy's parents. Each afternoon the teacher sent home with the boy papers with smiling faces stapled to them. Joe's parents reinforced the teacher's work by rewarding Joe with special treats at home for good work at school.

Social studies and science activities were whole-group activities in this first-grade classroom. Information was presented through films, slides, discussions, activities, field trips, and experiments. The only adaptations made by Mr. Thomas were to include Joe in a working group of able students who would assist him when needed and to have alternate assignments available when writing was demanded of the students.

For art and physical education, Mr. Thomas matched Joe with a "cooperative helper," a more able student who made sure Joe understood the directions. Mr. Thomas was also careful to use directions that were simply stated and were combined with demonstration.

Three times a week Mr. Thomas spent time working alone with Joe. For the first fifteen minutes of "Electric Company," Joe and Mr. Thomas reviewed Joe's work that day, including his work completed with the reading specialist. They completed data recording probes, and sometimes played a game.

Conclusion

By carefully assessing, programming, and evaluating Joe's performance, Mr. Thomas was able to slowly advance Joe's skills throughout the year. By carefully including Joe in classroom activities, Mr. Thomas made Joe feel good about his school work. Mr. Thomas helped Joe see that he could succeed if he tried.

References and Suggested Readings

Abeson, A. Education for handicapped children in the least restrictive environment. In M. Kindred, J. Cohen, D. Penrod, & T. Shaffer (Eds.), *The mentally retarded citizen and the law*. New York: The Free Press, 1976.

Affleck, J.Q., Lehning, T.W., & Brow, K.D. Expanding the resource concept: The resource school. *Exceptional Children*, 1973, *39*, 446-53.

American Journal of Mental Deficiency, November 1974, *79*, no. 3, 241-73.

Bateman, B. *The essentials of teaching*. San Rafael, Calif.: Dimensions Pub. Co., 1971.

Becker, W.C., Englemann, S., & Thomas, D.R. *Teaching 1: Classroom management*. Chicago: Science Research Associates, 1975.

Boehm, A.E. *The Boehm test of basic concepts*. New York: Psychological Corporation, 1971.

Brigance, A.H. *Inventory of basic skills*. Woburn, Mass: Curriculum Associates, 1977.

Brown v. *Board of Education* 347 U.S. 483 (1954).

Canter, L. & Canter, M. *Assertive discipline*. Los Angeles: Canter and Associates, 1976.

Chiba, C., & Semmel, M.I. Due process and least restrictive alternative: New emphasis on parental participation. In M.I. Semmel & J.L. Heinmiller (Eds.), *Viewpoints: The Education for All Handicapped Children Act (P.L. 94-142)—issues and implications*. Bloomington: School of Education, Indiana University, 1977.

Clark, D.C. *Using instructional objectives in teaching*. Glenview, Ill.: Scott, Foresman, & Company, 1972.

Diana v. *California State Board of Education*, Civil No. C-70-37, RFP N.D. Calif. (Feb. 5, 1970).

Dillman, C.M., & Rahmlow, H.F. *Writing instructional objectives*. Belmont, Calif.: Fearon Publishers, 1972.

Doll, E.A. *Measurement of social competence*. Circle Pines, Minn.: American Guidance Services, 1965.

Dunn, L.M. Special education for the mildly retarded: Is much of it justifiable? *Exceptional Children*, 1968, *35*, 5-22

Eicholz, R.E., O'Daffer, P.G., & Martin, E. *Elementary School Mathematics*. Mento, Calif.: Addison & Wesley, 1971.

Engelmann, S. *Preventing failure in the primary grades*. Chicago: Science Research Associates, 1969.

Federal Register, 42 (163) August, 1977, p. 42478

French, J.L. *Manual: Pictorial Test of Intelligence*. Boston: Houghton Mifflin, 1964.

Gardner, W.I. *Children with learning and behavior problems: A behavior management approach* (2nd ed.). Boston: Allyn & Bacon, 1978.

Gearheart, B.R. *The handicapped child in the regular classroom.* St. Louis: The C.V. Mosby Co., 1976.

Graubard, P.S. Children with behavioral disabilities. In L.M. Dunn (Ed.), *Exceptional children in the schools: Special education in transition* (2nd ed.). New York: Holt, Rinehart & Winston. 1973.

Grossman, H.J. (Ed.). *Manual on terminology and classification in mental retardation.* Washington, D.C.: American Association on Mental Deficiency, 1973.

Hallahan, D.P., & Cruickshank, W.M. *Psycho-educational foundations of learning disabilities.* Englewood Cliffs, N.J.: Prentice-Hall, 1973.

Hallahan, D.P., & Kauffman, J.M. *Exceptional children: Introduction to special education.* Englewood Cliffs, N.J.: Prentice-Hall, 1978.

Hammill, D.D., & Bartel, N.R. *Teaching children with learning and behavior problems* (2nd ed.). Boston: Allyn & Bacon, 1978.

Harris, A., & Clark, M.K. *New Macmillan reading program, Level 13.* New York: Macmillan, 1974.

Hewitt, F.M. *The emotionally disturbed child in the classroom.* Boston: Allyn & Bacon, 1968.

Howell, K.W., Kaplan, J.S., & O'Connell, C.Y. *Evaluating exceptional children: A task analysis approach.* Columbus, Ohio: Charles E. Merrill, 1979.

Joyce Z. No. 2035-60, C.C.P. Allegheny County, Pa. (1975).

Kauffman, J.M. *Characteristics of children's behavior disorders.* Columbus, Ohio: Charles E. Merrill, 1977.

Kirk, S.A. *Educating exceptional children.* Boston: Houghton Mifflin, 1962.

Krane, L. *Phonics is fun.* Cleveland, Ohio: Modern Curriculum Press, 1970.

Lovitt, T.C. *In spite of my resistance—I've learned from children.* Columbus, Ohio: Charles E. Merrill, 1977.

Lowenbraun, S., & Affleck, J.Q. Least restrictive environment. *Exploring Issues in the Implementation of P.L. 94-142.* Philadelphia, Pa.: Research for Better Schools Inc., 1978.

Makar, B.W. *Primary Phonics.* Cambridge, Mass.: Educators Pub. Service, Inc., 1974.

McCandless, B.R. Environment and intellectual functioning. In H.A. Stevens & R. Heber (Eds.), *Mental retardation: A review of research.* Chicago: University of Chicago Press, 1964.

McCarthy, J.J., & McCarthy, J.F. *Learning disabilities.* Boston: Allyn & Bacon, 1969.

Meyen, E.L. *Instructional based appraisal system (IBAS).* Bellevue, Wash.: Edmark Associates, 1976.

Mills v. *Board of Education of the District of Columbia.* 348 FSupp. 866, D.D.C. (1972).

National Association of State Directors of Special Education. *Functions of the placement committee in special education.* Washington, D.C. Author, 1976.

Novicky, W.N., Dorocak, S., Faulhaber, M.C. et al. *Growth in Spelling.* River Forest, Ill.: Laidlaw Brothers Publishers, 1975.

O'Leary, K.D., & O'Leary, G. *Classroom management: The successful use of behavior modification* (2nd ed.). New York: Pergamon Press, 1977.

Pasanella. A.L., & Volkmor, C.B. *Coming back. . . or never leaving: Instructional programming for handicapped students in the mainstream.* Columbus, Ohio: Charles E. Merrill, 1977.

Pennsylvania Association for Retarded Children v. *Commonwealth of Pennsylvania*, 334 F Supp. 1257, E.D. Pa. (1971).

Petreshene, S.S. *Complete guide to learning centers.* Palo Alto, Calif.: Pendragon House, 1978.

Popham, W.J. *The use of instructional objectives.* Belmont, Calif.: Fearon Publishers, 1973.

Popham, W.J. & Baker, E.L. *Planning an instructional sequence.* Englewood Cliffs, N.J.: Prentice-Hall, Inc., 1970.

Popham, W.J., & Baker, E.L. *Systematic instruction.* Englewood Cliffs, N.J.: Prentice-Hall, Inc., 1970.

Public Law 94-142. 94th Congress, S.6. (November 29, 1975).

Redd, W.H., Porterfield, A.L., & Anderson, B.L. *Behavior modification: Behavioral approaches to human problems.* New York: Random House, 1979.

Safford, P.L. *Teaching young children with special needs.* Saint Louis: C.V. Mosby, 1978.

Salvia, J., & Ysseldyke, J. *Assessment in special and remedial education.* Boston: Houghton Mifflin, 1978.

Shea, T.M. *Teaching children and youth with behavior disorders.* St. Louis: C.V. Mosby, 1978.

Smith, R.M., Neisworth, J.T., Greer, J.G. *Evaluating educational environments.* Columbus, Ohio: Charles E. Merrill, 1978.

Soskin, R.M. The least restrictive alternative: In principle and in application. *Amicus*, 1977, *2*, 28–32.

Stephanie L. No. J-184924 Juv. Div., C.C.P. Phila. County (1977).

Stephens, T.M. *Teaching skills to children with learning and behavior disorders.* Columbus, Ohio: Charles E. Merrill, 1977.

Stephens, T.M., Hartman, A.C., & Lucas, V.H. *Teaching children basic skills: A curriculum handbook.* Columbus, Ohio: Charles E. Merrill, 1978.

Sulzer, R., & Mayer, G.R. *Behavior modification procedures for school personnel* (2nd ed.). Hinsdale, Ill.: The Dryden Press, 1977.

Torres, S. (Ed.). *A primer on individualized education programs for handicapped children.* Reston, Va.: The Council for Exceptional Children, 1977.

Tracy, M.L., Gibbons, S., & Kladder, R.W. *Case conference: A simulation and resource book.* Bloomington, Ind.: Indiana Department of Public Instruction & Indiana University Developmental Training Center, 1976.

Turnbull, A.P. & Schulz, J.B. *Mainstreaming handicapped students: A guide for the classroom teacher.* Boston: Allyn & Bacon, Inc., 1979.

Turnbull, A.P., Strickland, B.B., & Brantly, J.C. *Developing and implementing individualized education programs.* Columbus, Ohio: Charles E. Merrill, 1978.

Wallace, G., & Kauffman, J.M. *Teaching children with learning problems* (2nd ed.). Columbus, Ohio: Charles E. Merrill, 1978.

Wallace, G., & Larsen, S. *Educational assessment of learning problems: Testing for teaching.* Boston: Allyn & Bacon, 1978.

Washington State Special Education Commission. *Directions in the education of handicapped children: A report to the Washington State Legislature.* Olympia, Wash.: January, 1974.

Wechsler, D. *Manual for the Wechsler Preschool and Primary Scale of Intelligence.* New York: Psychological Corporation, 1967.

White, O.R. & Haring, N.G. *Exceptional teaching: A multimedia training package.* Columbus, Ohio: Charles E. Merrill, 1976.

Wiederholt, J.L., Hammill, D.D., & Brown, V. *The resource teacher: A guide to effective practices.* Boston: Allyn & Bacon, 1978.

Worell, J., & Nelson, C.M. *Managing instructional problems: A case study workbook.* New York: McGraw-Hill, 1974.